A Journey To Love Energy

Embracing The Power Of Digital Healing Tones

ELYSE G. ROGERS

FEEL THE LOVE • FREE THE ENERGY • LOVE THE MUSIC • ELYSEMUSIC.COM

Dedicated to my Husband David (The Heyoka), for his unwavering commitment and continued support in this lifetime. He has shown me that 'real love' and soul mates do exist - may we continue to nurture each other's souls while enjoying endless moments of joy and laughter. I Love You x

To my Mum, who brought me into this world - thank you and I love you. And to 'H', for being the best Dad ever. 'I Miss you'.

To family, friends, colleagues, teachers, mentors, healers, and even exes—thank you for being a part of my journey and helping me become who I am today.

Gratitude to Sam, Morgane, my fans, online course members, and all past and present business mentors for their support in my solo music business. Thank you.

Big love to Twitch, Shiela, Lea, Sergio, Deyn, and all the other amazing musicians and artists out there. You make this world a better place for being in it.

I extend gratitude to all 90s music fans around the world for their unwavering support, Brandon for igniting this journey, and Jacques & Jordy @ International Artists for their assistance in securing global bookings, alongside my cherished 90s artist colleagues, reminiscing the friendship and joyous camaraderie backstage.

Special thanks to Rik Arron for his invaluable guidance and support, and to the entire crew at Story Terrace for helping bring this book to life and share it with the world.

CONTENTS

INTRO:
LOVE IS AN ENERGY!

Love, as we all know, is a force, and in today's fast-paced world, where self-care and a positive mindset are crucial to our wellbeing, we need it more than ever.

Referred to as 'the power of love', it is love in its purest form. It's the highest form of energy on Earth. It lifts us up. It transcends barriers, differences and breaks down walls of separation and creates bridges of connection. It can heal emotional wounds, dissolve conflicts, and transform individuals, relationships and communities.

Now, imagine a world bathed in love energy. What if love, joy, and peace overflowed in abundance, ready for us to tap into its boundless power? When was the last time you felt the warmth of love's embrace?

According to the Global Emotions Report 2022, one in four people experience deep sadness as part of their everyday lives, and in 2020, the world was the saddest, angriest, and most stressed out it's ever been. I don't know about you, but when I read this, it makes me feel really sad.

We have to ask ourselves, is it any wonder there is so much fear and sadness in the world? The major news channels worldwide tell us the worst things happening across the globe at any given moment, with some people using social media to criticise and judge each other, all within a broken system that continues to fuel and normalise addictions until our minds and bodies become unhealthy.

For too long, humanity has been stuck in a lower base energy, trapped by a powerful negative vibration grid wrapped around our world like prison bars. Each node and ley line point has been blocked and broken, keeping us all locked into hate and fear, unable to allow the love energy frequency to filter through to the Earth.

But hold on, because the universe is now beating to a brand new frequency, which has never been felt before. We're grooving to a new tune, with the vibrations of love, healing, and positivity.

Can you feel this new love vibration starting? I hope so because in this book, I'm turning up the volume on love energy, one frequency at a time!

MY MISSION

As a professional singer-songwriter, I've performed on big and small stages since the late eighties; whether it be stadiums, festivals, TV shows, radio stations, music videos, or meet and greets with fans all over the world, I've seen it all. Over time, my voice, stage image, and personal energy have changed a lot as I know firsthand how the music industry works, and how you need a lot of courage and wisdom to sustain it.

This book aims to share with you my transformative journey, from my departure from the music industry's toxicity during my peak of fame in the mid-90s to the discovery of a new way of expressing my voice and the benefits of using the different digital healing tones that I apply in my songs today. It's a journey back to my birth town of Manchester, UK roots, tracing my musical passion from childhood and the path that led me to my present state.

While you dive into these pages, you're already adding your magical touch to my mission of raising the planet's vibe to love through the power of positive music, just by being here and I can't thank you enough.

THE POWER OF POSITIVE MUSIC

In 2015, I released my first solo album, 'The Love Energy', which features nine songs that have been specifically tuned to the nine Solfeggio Tones. These healing and uplifting tones have been part of my life for the past 12 years – I love the fact that other people are just getting to know and use them now, which is something I talk about in this book.

The album is unique in that it is made up of positive, uplifting lyrics, my own timbre vocals, and in a pop and dance-genre style – all while using what I like to call 'digital healing tones.' It's like having a sound bath with gongs, tuning forks, chimes and crystal bowls, but through the online digital space!

There are many other tones outside of this standard set that I use in my music, one being 432 Hz, which is preferred by a lot of people who say that it's the 'Frequency of the Universe'. I personally prefer to tune my 9 tracked albums to the 9 Solfeggio tones, and then I use 432 Hz for my EP's and singles. I also work with different tones such as: 110 Hz, 111 to 999 Hz (Angel Frequencies), 295.8 Hz, binaural beats, and many more. Each of these tones works in different ways, individually unlocking the door to healing and transformation.

THE TWO MOST COMMON QUESTIONS
I GET ASKED ARE:

•Why do you write only positive lyrics in all of your songs?
•Why do you use digital healing tones in your music?

THE ANSWER IS SIMPLE...

Because I believe that most songs in the music charts today are lyrically disempowering, low in frequency and, therefore, affect our vibration. When I first discovered that the standard concert pitch for all instruments and music worldwide became 'tuned' to the frequency tone of 440 Hz in the 1950s, I wanted to know why. So I've been researching and sharing my knowledge about the many different digital tones ever since within my songs, my online course, and now this book.

WHAT DOES Hz MEAN?

Hertz (Hz) is the number of cycles of a sound wave that occur in one second, the speed at which a song goes around. The higher the number of Hz, the more cycles occur in one second.

WHY 440 Hz?

Known as the 'Standard Concert Pitch,' it's set worldwide. What this means is if a Pianist was playing in New York, and a Pianist was playing in London, they would both be playing the same pitch of 440 Hz (A above middle C) on a piano.

It was agreed and set by The Tavistock Institute in London, and the Rockefeller Foundation in New York, who would study and experiment with how we think, what music we listen to, and what cultural identities we identify with. It was used because it made people think and feel a certain way.

It has been proven that it conflicts with our human energy centers, from our hearts to the base of our spine. It stimulates ego and suppresses the heart-mind, intuition and creativeness. It has an avoidance affect on nature; it distorts and works on our left brain, the thinking part, to create 'boxed-in thinking', i.e. we all end up thinking the same.

In the late 1940s and early 50s Rock n Roll was linked with rebellion and rioting. Teenagers used to get into a frenzied state at a Beatles concert and there were always riots after a Rolling Stones show. 440 is extremely agitating to our human soul, and these kinds of things never happened before it was the norm.

THE 9 SOLFEGGIO FREQUENCIES

These healing tones are a sequence of nine frequencies that have been scientifically proven to promote healing and vitality for the conscious and unconscious mind. They have been used in spiritual music for centuries within churches to uplift the congregation and bring people closer to divine energy. The tones, each relating to a specific energy centre (or chakra) within the body, tap into our minds and bodies, sinking deep into the structure of our cells to heal us from the inside out. Literally blasting out any negative energy and replacing it with good.

THE 9 TONES, THEIR BENEFITS AND ENERGY CENTRES ARE:

1 174Hz – Security and Safety (Feet)

2 285Hz – Influences Energy Fields (Knees)

3 396Hz – Liberates Guilt and Fear (Root)

4 417Hz – Facilitates Change (Sacral)

5 528Hz – Transformation and Miracles (Solar Plexus)

6 639Hz – Reconnects and balances Relationships (Heart)

7 741Hz – Clear Communication and Self-expression (Throat)

8 852Hz – Transforms and Raises Awareness (Third Eye)

9 963Hz – Awakens Perfect State and Oneness (Crown)

SEE PAGE 12 FOR DIAGRAM CHART

My life has completely changed for the better since these powerful tones entered my world, so I have shared them in each of the nine chapters of this book.

WHAT ARE ENERGY CENTRES?

Energy Centres, also known as Chakras, act as internal and external portals of energy within your body's energy system. Influenced by daily activities and lifestyles, they naturally shift in and out of alignment. To maintain harmony in mind, body, and spirit, it's crucial to realign them. Luckily, with the power of healing tones, you can swiftly unblock and restore positive energy flow. Regular cleansing ensures a smoother flow, allowing these digital healing musical tones to effortlessly blast through and clear stagnant energies.

FOLLOW THE PATH OF LOVE

The question for you now is: Are you ready to embrace love energy and raise your vibration to love?

If you answered yes, then this is the book for you!

My intention is that this book will express my deep passion and enthusiasm for creating positive songs and how, by using the different digital healing tones, they can heal and empower you.

If you believe, like me, that the current music industry needs to upgrade and become a more positive role model for us and our children, then you are in the right place. But if you are content with how the music industry already does things, then it's important when reading this book to keep an open mind, to know that there is a future reality of a music industry that empowers and uplifts our mind, body and soul.

I know more recently that an energy of love has been filtering down and cleansing the planet like never before. Some individuals are calling it the 'love wave,' but I've known since 2011 that love energy was coming. So it seems timely to write and release this book now, it feels right.

HOW TO USE THIS BOOK

Not only is this book a story of my life (a mini-autobiography) it's also a workbook – just for you.

In each chapter, I share my journey, a tone, a reflection and a question, which will hopefully help you uncover where your energy is at and then upgrade you into a higher vibration.

I've also included a special gift just for you — a free 'book bonus' link in the resource section at the end of chapter 9, unlocking the magic of the 9 Solfeggio Tones. You can either listen to one frequency tone per chapter or wait until the end and listen to all of them. It's up to you.

Kindly note: If you have purchased this book, kindly keep this link for your personal use. Please refrain from sharing it with individuals who have not invested in this book, as creating and maintaining these resources requires time, energy, and financial investment on my part. Thank you for your understanding and support.

Before you begin, find yourself a quiet, comfortable reading place. Light your favourite candle. Put on some calming music and grab a notebook and pen (or use the space in the book provided). You may want to cleanse the area by playing a sound bowl, or you may prefer the silence; you can even light a stick of incense or white sage. Do what you need to do to feel relaxed and sink into your cosy space, making sure all electronic devices are turned off or muted for no distractions.

Thank you again, for embarking on this transformative journey with me. Your presence here signifies a resonance with the path we're about to walk together. As you delve into the following chapters, may my story and the power of these digital healing tones continue to elevate your spirit long after the book's pages have turned. May they light your soul up with love and expand your heart.

Together, let's raise the vibrational frequency of our world to love and make positive music the norm. It's the future.

Come with me now on A Journey To Love Energy...

With deepest gratitude,

Elyse
♥

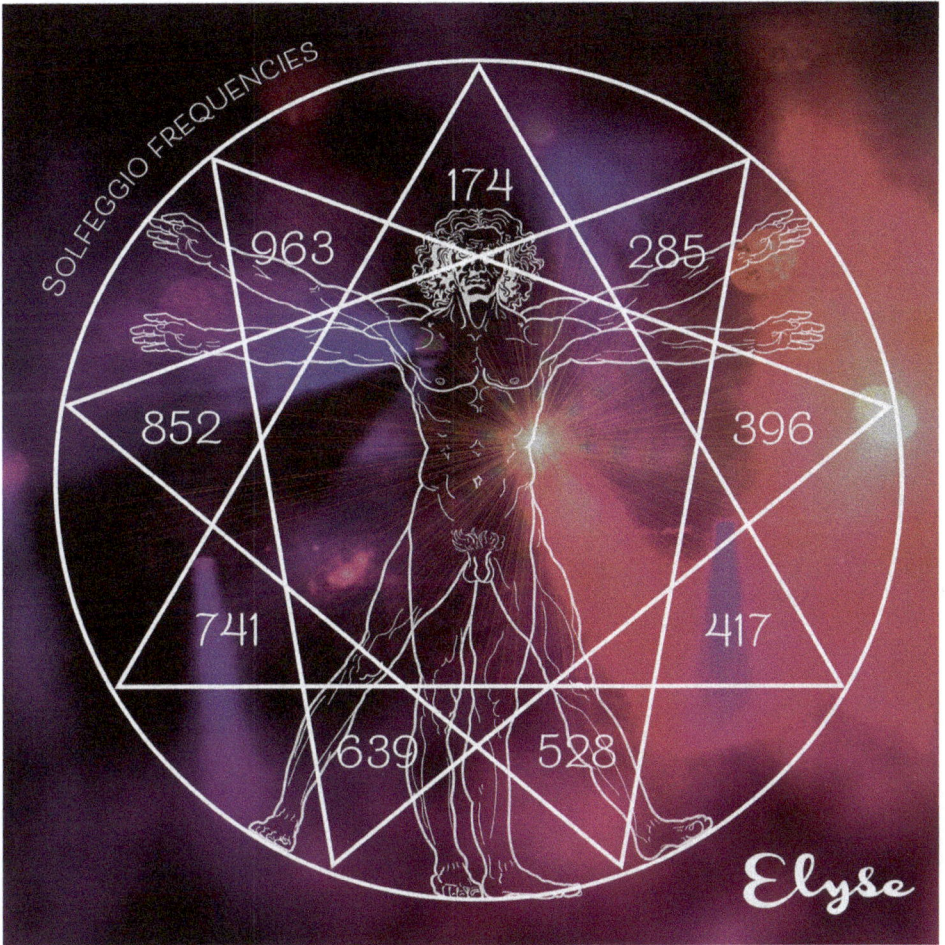

The Captivating Album Cover Of The 9 Solfeggio Frequencies

UNDERSTANDING ENERGY CENTRES

The 9 Energy Centres in your body are
which energy flows through

9. Crown
8. Third Eye
7. Throat
6. Heart
5. Solar Plexus
4. Sacral
3. Root
2. Knees
1. Feet

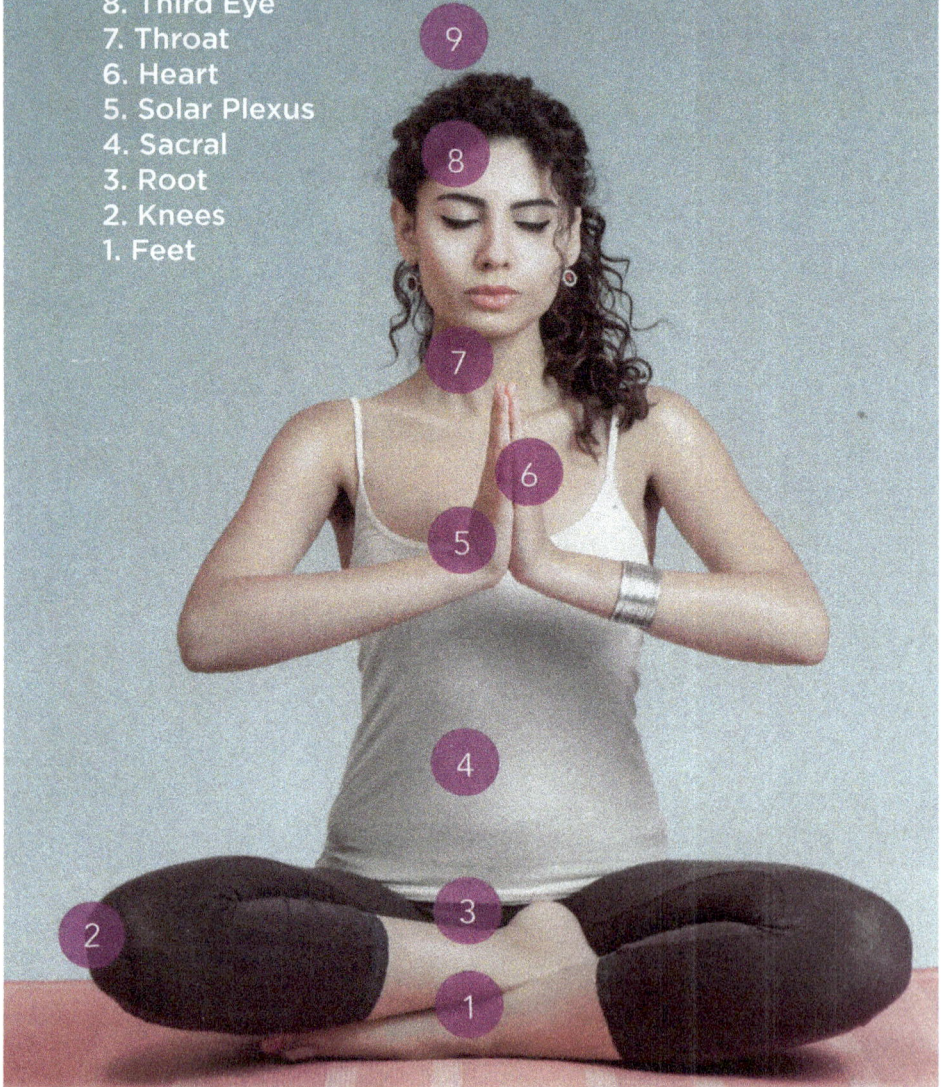

Chart Explaining The 9 Energy Centres Which Are Aligned With The 9 Solfeggio Tones

1

THE BEGINNING!

I was born Linda Carmen on Friday, 25th April 1969, at 5 p.m. in Withington Hospital, Manchester, England. My mother, Linda Mary, (who I like to call 'mum'), was a fair skin, blue-eyed, blonde-haired English rose, while my father, Antonio Joseph (nickname: Pepe), was a tanned dark-haired, Spaniard.

I have always been full of life and spirit – since before I even came out of the womb. In the final moments of my mum's pregnancy with me, she walked to the doctor's surgery about 10 minutes away, without even knowing her waters had broken! She was very much in labour before the ambulance even arrived – I was very keen to enter this world. It was a quick labour, weighing 7lbs 5oz. She named me after her – or, as I became known, Little Linda.

As a child growing up in South Manchester, I remember feeling rooted in those urban streets. My youngest days were very active and playful: I was an only child but had an Alsatian puppy dog that was like a sister to me. Ketty and I were very close. We had brought her down from an American Military Base in Dunoon, Scotland, from my Auntie

Maria (Pepe's sister), who was married to an American marine stationed there. Ketty was a trained military pup but failed the last dog training test, so she couldn't be used and had to go to a good family home instead. I was a newborn when my parents got her, but they knew she'd be the perfect companion for me. Ketty was such a solid sweet, caring beautiful-natured dog; we did everything together. I remember I used to lie on the living room floor, face to face, squeezing right up to her wet, healthy nose and singing to her – my very first audience. But when I was 13, she had a mini-stroke and I took one week off school to hand-feed her by the side of my bed. She recovered and lasted another two years, sadly passing at age 15. I have so many fond memories of our time together. She was a blessing.

I was always very active as a child – dancing and full of playful energy. At one point, I had an enormous wooden rocking horse that I rode back and forth, which Mum said I went "crazy" on. I remember I used to try and get the horse's nose to hit the floor in front of me, and then I would hurl it back up again so the tail would hit the ground behind me. I rocked it so hard that my Mum was scared I'd fly off it and so she decided to remove it. She bought me a child's blue nurse's outfit and a doll for Christmas that year instead – something that couldn't cause too much damage.

Mum and Pepe lived in Stretford for a short while, before moving to a nice big house in Taunton Road, Sale. Pepe had first come to the UK because he had a trial at Peterborough

FC. When his footballing career didn't work out, he opened up his own restaurant – Al Patio – which ended up being quite successful.

When I was four years old, tragically, my lovely English grandma Beattie passed away - shockingly, she was only 44 years of age, so sadly, I don't remember her very much, and soon after that happened my parents separated. My mum who has strong work ethics even to this day, opened up her first café bar, called Shop and Grill on Fog Lane in Didsbury. The café, with its big tables, brightly coloured orange seats and a large coffee bar sign, was on one side of the shop, with a delicatessen on the other side, selling a varied selection of different meats and cheese, and a large chicken rotisserie oven in the front shop window. Aged just 25, and with a small child, she ran Shop and Grill all by herself. How she did it still amazes me to this day. She had so much energy and amazing natural business skills – running from one side of the shop to the other to serve customers (before she employed any staff) that over the next 14 years, her resourcefulness and flexibility made the cafe a huge success.

I knew every inch of that cafe. We lived in the small two-bedroom apartment above it until I was 10 years old, so much of my childhood was spent there. I went to school, but otherwise, I was at the café – helping behind the counter, wrapping up knives and forks in paper napkins, clearing tables and nattering away with the regulars. It was a challenge for my mother, that was for sure: she worked from 7 a.m.

to 7 p.m. most days, six days a week, but there was always an extra-tasty Sunday dinner every weekend, and we would always enjoy a fresh cabbage sandwich, made on thick white bread slices, with salt and real butter before our dinner whilst waiting for the meal to cook, and then for dessert - orange jelly, tinned mixed fruit cocktail and vanilla custard trifle with whipped double cream and sprinkles – it was heaven!

I was always very lively as a child – while I wasn't very academic, I was super creative, sporty and gifted at art and music. I loved drawing and painting, but was really good at anything outdoors. I was on most school sports teams and would compete in the Manchester District 100m race, relay race, and cross country. I was also excellent at directions. One day, my mum dropped me off in her car at All Saints Primary School and went home, but when I got to the main school gates, they were closed (it was a bank holiday, and she did not know) – so I had to make my own way back! I was only four years of age, and I remember trying to cross the busy road, and after some time, a car did eventually stop for me, and I was able to find my own way back all by myself because I'd memorised the route, the roads, the houses and the field where we would walk my dog, Ketty, every day. I was always determined, even at this young age. Something similar happened again one summer when I visited Spain while on a boat trip from England with my parents. I somehow went missing! Aged just three years of age, I had made my own way back down to the cabin for a nap, without telling anyone. I remember going down a long corridor and it being similar but not our room. So I tried again and found it. My mum was so shocked (and relieved) when she found me sitting on the cabin bed.

At age seven – mine and my mum's lives were about to change forever. Harry lived just off Fog Lane. He had emigrated in the late 1960s to Australia when he was a young 21-year-old man with four of his good friends. Back then, shipping companies like P&O and Orient Line were taking British migrants over to live between 1945 and 1972 for only ten British pounds. He returned back to the UK, six years later to help his mother out, as his father had taken ill at that time.

Back in Manchester, at age 28, Harry was a self-employed window cleaner and came into Shop and Grill cafe one day, to ask my mother if she wanted the shop windows cleaned. From that moment, Harry was smitten with her.

I remember the first time I met him. It was late one night, and he had been on a date with my mum, and they sat chatting on the settee. I woke up and walked into the apartment living room and he was so friendly and kind to me, I will never forget it. For many years, I called him 'H', but eventually, I would give him Father's day cards and presents, and write Dad inside. He would bring me small bags of mixed sweets from the local sweet shop, he taught me how to play snooker, darts, and board games like Monopoly and Scrabble - he was also good with playing cards and would even teach me magic tricks. I remember once he got me a secondhand chopper bike, and we sprayed it sky blue (like his favourite

Manchester City football team colours), put two long plastic white tassels onto each side of the handlebars, and neon coloured spoke straws in the wheels.

Around the age of eight, I had to take three weeks off school as I came down with a major case of chicken pox. During this time, I found myself confined to the settee, wrapped in blankets, hugging a hot water bottle watching daytime TV. I had an itchy rash all over my entire body, mainly my chest and back, but the worst was on my face. The tiny blisters were very stressful, and I was in complete agony, I was burning up in temperature due to the high fever and I cried a lot. I still have a small scar on the top of my right cheek today from that testing period.

To soothe myself, I was given large bottles of a famous energy drink that was the go-to remedy for ailments in the 70s and was thought to help you recover quickly in times of sickness.

However, as I recovered and returned to my usual routine, I unintentionally developed a taste for fizzy drinks, sweets, and junk food. This newfound love for indulgent treats became an enduring part of my youth, and although I was sporty as a child, the excess weight pilled on, and I became uncomfortable in my own body.

Soon after my tenth birthday, the three of us and Ketty moved to a new home on Saddlewood Avenue in East Didsbury about one mile from Shop and Grill, where I would make new friends and start a brand new high school.

MUSIC AND ME

Music was a big love of mine – I had fallen in love with songs at a very young age, as there was always music being played either in the home, the car and even the cafe. From Elvis to The Everly Brothers and even country and western, I had heard them all because as a teenager, every Saturday after working at the cafe, I would walk straight to Sifters record shop on Fog Lane and buy the latest chart single or album. I was obsessed with records and knew a lot about music, the charts and band names and their songs. It was often said that I should have been a female DJ, because I had amassed such a huge record collection of 7, 10 and 12 inch records and vinyl.

One summer though when I was 14, I was sitting on the playground swings in Fog Lane Park with my friend at the time when two local boys struck up a conversation with us. It turned out we were all really passionate and interested about making music, so we decided there and then that the four of us would form a band together, so we did. Our group consisted of a lead singer, a bass player, a drummer and I would play keyboard and do backing vocals. I remember walking home that night across the park field feeling excited about this new musical adventure. It had happened so quickly, and it felt so powerful.

We would practise three times a week in a rehearsal room, and it was great fun, for we were all teenagers and it kept us safe and off the streets – I still have some of those songs on cassette. The band that began with only four, ended up eventually with eight members. Adding a sax player, percussionist, lead guitarist and another singer. We were the most passionate bunch ever – it felt like nothing could stop us, fuelled by milk chocolate digestive biscuits and strong cups of milky English tea in our break times, we loved it!

Despite the huge amount of energy I had growing up, I was actually quite shy during my teenage years, as I would use my long black wavy hair to cover my face and wore baggy clothes hoping no one would see me. But I absolutely loved writing songs. We covered famous 80s artists such as Alison Moyet and Sade, as well as lots of soul and funk tracks, playing at local community centres and small music festivals. Up on those stages, I felt a great sense of belonging and was even able to write my own music, which was something that felt incredibly powerful to me. The song lyrics I wrote back then used to be about rejected love, abandoned love, looking for love – basically I was looking for someone outside of myself to love me: this is very different to the songs I write today, but I didn't know any better then because I was used to the music industry feeding me that same narrative at the time, so it felt normal to write like that.

Yes, the songs were quite sad and disempowering, but I found songwriting to be an outlet for my self-expression and the feelings I felt being an introverted teenager; plus, it was a huge laugh, and I just loved having so much fun with my friends.

A good sound foundation was set in my childhood, for I was lucky to have found my passion, and my love for music as a child. I always used to say music was 'therapeutic' - a bit like writing this book.

The first digital healing tone is 174 Hz, is based at the feet energy centre, and is all about 'Security and Safety.' This tone is best for enhancing feelings of stability, helping you to ground and create a strong foundation. Reflect: Begin by remembering your childhood and what gave you a sense of security and comfort. Consider how you can further create a sense of grounding and safety.

Use the space here to write (or in your journal) about your own beginnings, with family, friends, animals, and even what your environment was like. What foundations did you build from, and how did your early childhood shape you? What thoughts, ideas, and insights came up for you while reading this chapter?

_____

_____

_____

_____

_____

_____

Innocence Captured! My Debut Into The World – First Baby Photo!

Throwback to 70s Charm: Mum And Me In A Retro Photo Booth

Bonding Bliss: Moments with My Loyal Dog Companion, Ketty

Festive Fun: Wearing My Nurses Outfit - Christmas Present

Discover Culinary Delights At 'Shop & Grill' On Fog Lane –
My Mum's First Café And Deli Bar!

2

SINGING & AMERICA!

By the time I was 18 in 1987, the band had dispersed, but my enthusiasm for music had not left with it.

I decided to sign up for private 1-1 classical singing lessons in Cheadle with a professional classical music tutor. At the time, I was working full-time as a secretary for a computer company, so some of my monthly wages got invested into those singing lessons, which I felt was so worth it. I trained in Classical Italian for one year, and it was my initial intention to learn breathing techniques and better diction. One day, my teacher told me that I would make a great Soprano. I was honoured she would make such a positive remark to me, as she was very busy and a well-respected tutor, until she mentioned that it would take me 10 years to fully train and become professional.

This felt like such a long time. Too long. I was young and full of energy, and I was looking to get going with my life; I didn't want to wait 10 years.

Instead, I saw a newspaper advertisement for a band in Warrington looking for a female singer. The group was called 'Remix', and they covered hit songs by Phil Collins,

Bryan Adams, and many other chart artists from that era. I decided to audition and went to the Cherry Tree pub, where the band had hired out a large, empty function room at the back. One of the band members had sent me a cassette with three songs to learn for the audition a few weeks earlier. I had rehearsed them all, and wrote down all the lyrics on an A4 pad, so I was well prepared. This was the decade of big hair and big perms! However, I looked very different from all the long-haired blonde girls also auditioning in the same room. I had recently modelled for Vidal Sassoon hairdressers in Manchester City Centre and had been given a cropped bob hairstyle to shoulder length, but my hair is semi-wavy and would just curl up at the ends, so I went back again just before the audition, to have it all shaved off at the sides, and cut super short into a ' pixie' style. (Unbeknown to me, I had this 'pixie' hairstyle for the next 18 years, until I was 36). I was the only one in the audition room with short dark hair. I stood out. When I sang, I also flipped the lyrics around, because the three songs I had to learn were sung by men to women, so I made sure I was singing words to a man. Example: I love her, I changed to I love him. I was so surprised that no one else did this because it was completely natural for me to change the words. I think it was a test on the band members' part, to see how smart we were. Soon after the audition, I got offered the job. Remix travelled all over the North West of England, to Widnes, Liverpool, Manchester and even as far as Anglesey, in Wales. We played all the social clubs and bingo halls as the first act from 8 – 9 pm, with a second set later on that evening. The rooms would be swirling with cigarette smoke (it was legal to smoke in clubs back then), so when I arrived home at 3 o'clock in the morning after my gig, I smelled like an ashtray. My hair, my clothes and even my skin would smell of cigarettes, so the first thing I would do is jump in the shower, get my PJs on, and make some warm toast with butter on. My mother would always wait up for me, and we'd sit and chat with a nice cup of strong milky tea and a hot water bottle (if it was wintertime).

As payment, I received only £20 for each gig, so the money made was never split evenly or fairly– this, I found out later, was a recurring theme across the music industry. I ended up leaving Remix within the year.

AMERICA, HERE I COME!

Shortly afterward, I wanted a change, so I left for Boston, Massachusetts, where I was an au pair for nine weeks over the summer holidays.

Before I left the UK, I worked three jobs to save money for my trip. I worked full-time as a marketing assistant in an estate agent's, Monday to Friday, two nights a week as a salesperson selling newspapers over the phone, and three nights a week as a barmaid in a pub. I managed to save £1,000, which would give me extra spending money, as I intended to stay two extra weeks after my work had finished with a flight down to Florida.

I boarded a Delta Airlines flight from Manchester to New York and stayed at the Roosevelt Hotel in Manhattan. The next morning, I was greeted by the host, and we took a flight to Boston.

The American family had hired me to be a live-in nanny for their three-year-old twin girls. I quickly settled into family life as a short-term family member, I had my own bedroom with queen size bed, a big wardrobe and a bathroom with a double sink. I ate all my meals with the family and received weekly pocket money of £15.

They had an enormous, beautiful house (the girls' clothes, toys, and bedrooms were an overload of bright pink and purple colour) and a double garage with an electric key fob that I was super impressed with because I didn't have to get out of the car to open the garage door. Every weekend we'd go to their stunning lake house with a man-made beach, on Lake Winnipesaukee, New Hampshire, where they taught me how to water ski on their small speed boat. On one occasion, there was a visit by the family's brother, his wife and two children, who had hired a German au pair for that summer and brought her along for the weekend. We were both asked to water ski, and I found out later that there was a gamble within the family to see who would ski better - the English girl or the German girl? Thankfully, I did ski really well, as my host family had previously given me some private lessons, but the German girl was a natural snow skier, so she struggled to even get the skis out of the water. She kept pointing her ski's down in the water, so could not lift up. I won the bet – the family loved me for it! We all got on so well – except my Manchester accent was quite strong, so the twins didn't understand me at first when I would read them bedtime stories.

Sundays were my day off, so they always gave me the family's automatic car to drive to the nearest town. I went to the cinema and explored the local area, even though I did get pulled over by the police one night for not having my full light beams on after I had been watching the latest movie!

After my job was finished, I went to Florida for a few weeks to stay with friends working at Disney World, then headed back to the UK. Before I left though, I was given Pepe's phone number from someone who knew him as he was living nearby with his new family since emigrating to the States a few years earlier. We spoke on the phone for a short while and agreed to meet up, but unfortunately it was not to be, and It would be another thirty years until I would speak with him again.

Back in England, I returned to my secretarial work. I feel like I worked non-stop in those years – driven by my mother's incredible work ethic – to make money so that I could travel and keep having fun. I had also gone back to singing lessons, but this time I had lessons with the famous Sheila Gott in Stockport, who is an incredible vocalist and had been the original voice for a famous UK cartoon television show theme tune. She was on the social club circuit, singing Motown and other 60s songs. She took me out (into the wild!) to train and mentor me, allowing me to perform vocal harmonies in the clubs alongside her.

I remember one time we were singing together at Denton West End Social Club and I noticed at the back of the room there was a man who had both his hands held over his ears and had a painful look on his face. It put me off singing, and I forgot the words to my song. When we finished the show, Sheila asked me what had happened. I told her about the man, and that I had got distracted as I saw he was protecting his ears while I was singing.

As we were leaving the building, she asked me to show her where the man had been sitting. As we walked to the back of the large hall, she said, 'Look, there's a big music speaker here high up on the wall; it was above his head. He was putting his hands over his ears to protect them because the sound system was too loud, not because he did not like your singing.' I cringed with embarrassment and felt silly that I had even considered such a thing. It was a lesson learned.

It's not uncommon for singers to experience a lack of confidence or self-doubt. It's a natural part of the creative process. If only I knew this was normal at such a young age and that it would change with time and experience.

Singing became my whole life again, and I felt so happy. But then my life suddenly took its next big turn, which was to put me on a whole new path. I was about to move nearly 800 miles, away from my beloved Manchester, and away from everything I'd known before.

It was in the summer of 1992, and I moved to Germany.

The second digital healing tone is 285 Hz, is based at the knee energy centre, and is all about 'Influencing Energy Fields.' This tone harmonises your auric field, helping you to achieve physical and emotional well-being. It enhances overall vitality and energy flow.

Reflect: Imagine your energy field right now is clean and purified. How can you create good energy flow through your energy field right now?

Use the space here to write (or in your journal) about any training you took or would like to take to enhance your life. Who has been a positive role model and mentor to you? What thoughts, ideas, and insights came up for you while reading this chapter?

_____

_____

_____

_____

_____

_____

_____

Cherished Moments: Capturing the Trio – Me, Harry, and Mum

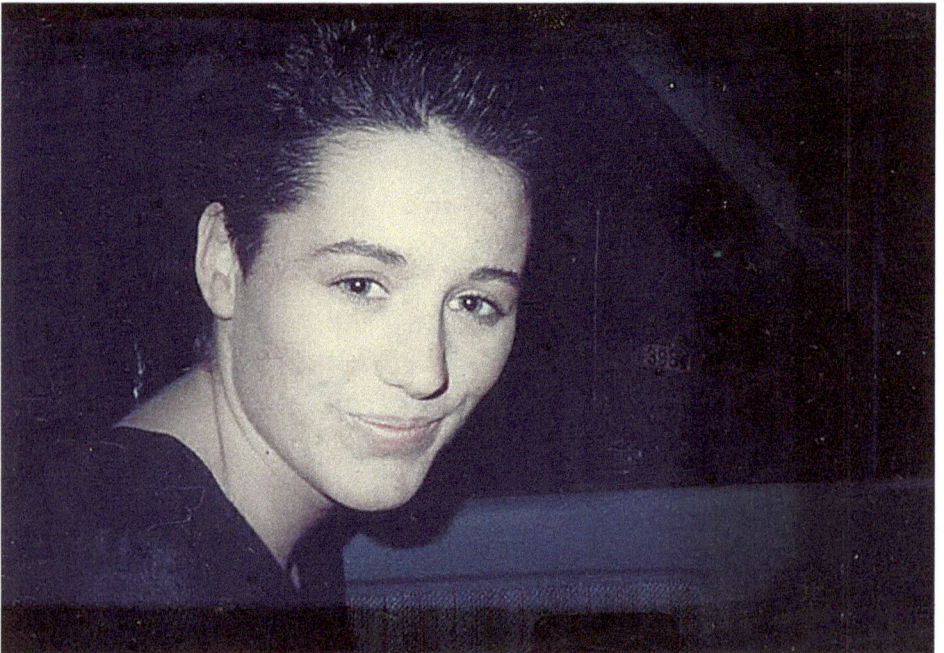

Embracing Independence: Young, Free, and Single at 18!

3

GERMANY &
THE RECORD DEAL!

At the ripe age of 21, I boarded a ship from Hull to Rotterdam that would carry me to a new life in Germany.

As the ship's horn echoed across the harbour, my heart raced with anticipation. I ran outside to the main deck and saw my mum and Harry on the shoreline, waving frantically. Their teary eyes mirrored my own mixed emotions. It was a bittersweet farewell, a moment that marked both an ending and a beginning.

I can still see them both giving a final wave of encouragement and love. As the shore grew smaller as the ship sailed away, I couldn't help but wonder about the adventures that awaited me. Little did I know that this journey would shape my life in ways I could never have imagined and that the memories of that day would remain etched in my heart forever.

Imagine a young Mancunian lass, brimming with dreams and a suitcase filled with English tea bags, landing in Germany. I had no idea how to say 'Guten Tag,' let alone navigate the challenging world of living abroad at such a young age.

As I reflect on those early days, it's clear that taking the plunge so young and moving abroad was a life-changing decision and a very bold move. I took full-time jobs as a civilian secretary working within the British Army, which involved a range of different tasks crucial for the smooth operation of different military units within both the ambulance and police regiments.

Beyond my day-to-day work, I dedicated myself to physical fitness. Each day, I would go on an energetic physical workout routine that included either running, swimming or weight training. This commitment to fitness was not just a personal choice but an embodiment of the discipline and resilience I had acquired over time.

One memory of my daily routine was a 6-mile run I undertook after work. Starting each morning with my backpack on, I was dropped off at my workplace. At the end of the day, I would lace up my running shoes and run the journey back home, covering the entire distance on foot. On other days, I would go out during my lunch break into the German forest, which was filled with a mixture of pine, beech, and oak trees, with my headphones on, listening to uplifting music on my walkman. These were good days.

On 3rd June 1993, I joined a talent show called 'Search For The Stars'. The finals were held on a military base, and it was organised by the British Forces Broadcasting Station

(BFBS). I'd entered the singing competition because I was missing using my creativity, and I just loved performing live so much, so to my huge surprise (and complete delight) I ended up coming in third place in the semi-finals – I was through to the finals! The full-day event was split into two halves, sections of ten acts (twenty acts in total ranging from soloists, duos and bands), with a break in between the performances. It's common knowledge in the competition world that anyone who performs in the first half of a show like this would be forgotten about by the end of the competition because there were so many other acts, and so, therefore, wouldn't be in with a chance of winning. I was lucky because I was to perform at the beginning of the second act.

It was now my turn, as I stood up and walked behind the heavy stage curtains to the right-hand side of the stage, ready to take my turn and do what I had trained for. I remember waiting alone for about 5 minutes (which seemed more like 20 minutes) and silently taking deep breaths and praying. I remember standing in between two large, heavy grey metal doors that were open wide to an outside back open field. It had been a warm day and the cool breeze was filtering in nicely, and all I could see as I looked up to the early evening night sky were thousands of bright twinkling stars. I asked God right there and then for inner- strength, for me to remember all my lyrics, to come in the top three, and overall for me to have fun and enjoy myself. My turn arrived. I took a deep breath and stepped onto the stage.

I stood up in front of the seven judges who sat at the back of the room on a long table, a mixture of military personnel and radio DJs, as I smiled like crazy and sang my heart out. I had chosen two songs to sing, '1-2-3' by Gloria Estefan and 'Saving The Best Till Last' by Vanessa Williams. I wore a short black fitted dress which had a mixture of funky bright neon colours splattered all over it, black ankle boots, big hooped silver earrings, bright pink lipstick, and with my short black pixie hairstyle, I was ready to go. I knew I stood a chance because we were not just being judged on our singing ability and talent but on our stage outfit, image and personality as well. I had an excellent time, throwing my soul into those songs and giving a performance to be proud of.

After time conferring, the judges announced the winners. I came 2nd overall and won a silver clock trophy and 750 Deutschmarks in cash. It was said by the compere when he announced the winning order that I should have won by far as there were only 3 points between the military guy who won and me. I later found out that the winner had a member of his family and a work colleague on the judging panel. But to me, I was happy for my 2nd place because I knew I had done it all myself, and my wish had come true.

Soon after this, I was invited to a US military camp in Frankfurt to sing and meet with some of the winners from the American camp competition. Something inside me knew this was an incredible opportunity. I felt like I was at the start of something big and willed this chance into being with all my might. I knew I was a singer at heart. So, I decided to take action and make it happen.

On 24th September 1993, I wrote a letter to one of the Radio DJ judges who'd been on the judging panel, offering to write and sing jingles. Shortly afterwards, I received a callback and I was asked to write a jingle for his lunchtime radio show. I began writing a few different jingles, and he was very impressed. Soon after working with him, he told me he had sent a demo tape to a big record label.

Sony was interested in me as an artist. They wanted to offer me a solo record deal!

I really felt that I had manifested this into being. I felt filled with abundance, and was attracting opportunities to me like a magnet.

Then, that same week something else happened.

Another chance rolled out before me.

It felt like fate.

The third digital healing tone is 396 Hz, is based at the root energy centre, and is all about 'Liberating Guilt and Fear.' This tone assists with eliminating negative emotions and reducing stress and anxiety.

Reflect: Visualise your life filled with calm, positivity, and high self-esteem. How do you release negative emotions, stress and anxiety?

Use the space here to write (or in your journal) about any negative feelings or memories you now wish to release. What are the best things to do when dealing with stress or anxiety? What thoughts, ideas, and insights came up for you while reading this chapter?

_____

_____

_____

_____

_____

_____

_____

_____

_____

_____

_____

_____

_____

_____

Unleashing Glamour: Embracing the Charm on My First Professional Photoshoot

Nostalgic Flashback: 1994 Snapshot with Sheila Gott and Me!

4

CATS & BECOMING FAMOUS!

O ut of the blue, I received a phone call from an English music producer living in Berlin. He said he was a songwriter for a new group looking for a female vocalist and asked if I would be interested in applying for the role. I sent my CV, radio jingles on a cassette and a couple of professional photographs in the first class post. One week later, he phoned me again and invited me to fly to Berlin for an audition, which went well.

Soon after, I had a big life decision to make. Do I go solo, or join the group?

This was a pivotal crossroads in my life, a moment that would forever alter the course of my music career. It was a choice between two promising opportunities: a solo deal that tempted me with the appeal of freedom and self-expression, or a group deal that had already started its ascent into the German music charts, promising a quicker path to stardom.

One evening, after a particularly demanding day, I found myself physically and emotionally drained. Seeking solace and clarity, I decided to unwind in a warm, soothing bubble bath. As the water enveloped me, the weight of this huge decision pressed heavily upon my heart and mind. The bathroom became a sanctuary, the only space where I could escape the outside world and confront my inner turmoil. I cried a lot. I wanted to make the right choice, as I had been working towards this moment for a long time, and they were both great opportunities.

With eyes closed, I submerged myself in thought, reflecting on the pros and cons of each path. I knew the solo deal represented the freedom to craft my music in my own unique way, an artistic canvas on which I could paint my emotions and experiences. However, it also came with the risk of non-recognition and more of a risk.

On the other hand, the group deal came with the promise of immediate exposure, as the charts had already embraced their music. It seemed like a shortcut to fame, but it also meant compromising on creative autonomy, as the group dynamic demanded a harmonious blend of voices and music style in a genre of music I had never really worked in before. I would be working with a male rapper, and this was certainly different for me.

As I lay there in the bath, the water serving as both a comfort and a metaphor for the ebb and flow of life's choices, I struggled with uncertainty. I knew that the answer had to come from within. It was my decision as to which path I would choose.

With much thought, I decided I was going to be in the signed band with the male rapper. The group was called

MAXX, and they already had a song in the charts called 'Get-A-Way.' This was 1994, and I quickly slipped into the new role and recorded a new song at my first audition in the Berlin recording studio – the second single – 'No more (I can't stand it).' Our management told me to be patient as we had to wait a few months for things to start moving. Live shows, radio and TV interviews, photo shoots, and music videos needed to be booked.

During those transitional moments when I was waiting for my music career to take off, my life was blessed by the presence of two beloved short-haired cats, Lewis, a black and white male, and Cleo, a female tabby. These feline companions became my loyal confidantes, offering comfort and support during the uncertain twists and turns in my journey.

Caring for them was not just a responsibility; it was a heartwarming bond that added depth and richness to my days. They were a source of unconditional love and a reassuring presence as I navigated the uncertainty of the music world.

One happy memory that stood out during this time was the ingenious use of my old dog whistle. This whistle, originally used for my Alsatian dog, Ketty, found a new purpose in my life. With patience and a bit of training, I managed to teach the cats to respond to the sound of that dog whistle. The sharp, distinct tone of the whistle became a call to them, an invitation to come indoors and join me in the coziness of our home.

I recall one early evening, I decided to visit the local army NAFA store, which was based on a military camp right behind my house. As I approached the entrance, something caught my eye – my faithful feline companion, Lewis, had decided to join me on this little adventure.

The soldier standing guard with his rifle across his chest at the entrance was, to say the least, utterly flabbergasted. I couldn't help but smile as I walked past him with Lewis confidently trailing behind. This was a sight to behold, and it seemed to defy all conventional expectations. A cat, in the midst of a military base, trotting along and showing no ID card to enter.

Inside the shop, I went about my shopping, enjoying the idea that Lewis was somewhere nearby. When I had gathered all that I needed, I made my way back outside, and then it was time to put Lewis's special talent on display.

With a twinkle in my eye, I gave a distinctive whistle, the same one that had previously summoned him so faithfully. To my delight, he came bounding towards me from around the back of the building, where he had been waiting patiently. The amazement in the eyes of the guard was undeniable. He watched in astonishment as Lewis, with his furry tail held high, joined me on the pedestrian crossing with feline elegance, strolling in perfect sync, his little paws tracing the painted lines on the road.

The guard, still wide-eyed and utterly shocked, couldn't

help but voice his disbelief, "I have never seen a cat do that before!" It was a moment of shared laughter and joy, as we both marveled at Lewis's exceptional and unexpected talent for following instructions and being quite human-like, even on a military base.

The memory of that day remains a sweet memory in my mind of how our furry friends can surprise us with their unique and endearing quirks. And how love is a great communicator between humans and animals.

CHART SUCCESS!

It was such an exciting time, and I felt like I was constantly pinching myself - it was so surreal. I remember the management telling me that when things did eventually take off I would be begging them for a day off. It was true.

The very early days of my music career were filled with excitement and much anticipation, and a pivotal moment in that journey was when I received another invitation to fly to Berlin to go for my first big photoshoot. It wasn't just any photo shoot; it was an opportunity to showcase my unique style and identity as an emerging artist. The stage clothes carefully selected for the occasion were more than just garments; they were an extension of my creative expression. Dressed in vivid, 90s-inspired clothing– featuring a vibrant orange and yellow combo, paired with sleek black knee-length boots – and highlighted by a bold swipe of vibrant red lipstick, the scene was undeniably a tribute to the era.

The day of the photo shoot was a whirlwind of activity. A dedicated team of professionals worked tirelessly to capture my persona through the lens. The camera clicked and flashed, freezing moments that would become iconic images.

Alongside the photo shoot, the trip to Berlin also brought forth a series of interviews. Radio stations and magazine companies were eager to get to know the story of my journey and my inspirations. It was a whirlwind of discussions, and a chance to share my passion and vision with a wider audience.

This journey to Berlin marked the beginning of something big. The memories of that trip, the photo shoot, and the interviews remain etched in my mind as the stepping stones to a music career that would soon take me to even greater heights.

The year was 1994, a pivotal moment in my music career. We achieved remarkable chart success with our first single, 'Get-A-Way,' which soared to the number one position in Greece and reached the top ten in the European charts, marking our international breakthrough. The UK charts also recognised our music, granting us a respected number three position.

Our second single, 'No More, I Can't Stand It' continued to cement our place in the music industry. It reached the number one spot in Finland and secured a number eight position in the UK.

As our journey progressed, the release of our third single,

'You Can Get It,' brought its own share of success with a number twenty-one position in the UK charts.

Complementing our string of hit singles, was the album - 'To The Maxximum.' This album became a significant milestone in my career, showcasing a collection of different songs such as: Heart of Stone, Fight and Ritmo De La Casa.

Creating music videos in different locations added a cool dimension to my music career, too, with Marseille in the South of France, Budapest in Hungary and Manhattan in New York. Each location brought its own distinct personality to the music videos, enhancing the visual storytelling and allowing me to connect with audiences across the world.

The year 1994 was an unforgettable chapter in my musical journey, which I feel so privileged to have experienced. It was marked by chart-topping achievements and the release of a well-received album.

Things moved super fast, and we were asked to sing on Top of the Pops, the UK's biggest mainstream music TV show at that time. We flew first class to London and filmed the live performance in the daytime. The show would also feature some big named acts, such as: The Brand New Heavies, Wet Wet Wet, and Level 42. I also remember having a great chat with Ant and Dec outside the makeup room. It was a fantastic day!

I had dreamt of this my entire life - the chance to perform on Top of the Pops. But as I stood backstage, the excitement was tinged with fear. This iconic show, one I had watched faithfully since I was a small child, was not just any performance. It was live.

In my anxious state, while waiting off stage, I found myself standing next to a security guard who must have sensed my nervousness. With a warm smile, he handed me an extra-strong mint, a simple gesture that carried a world of comfort. As I let the mint dissolve on my tongue, I couldn't help but feel a bit more grounded, a bit more ready to face the bright lights and the millions of viewers.

With minutes to go before my cue, I stepped outside for a moment of solace and telephoned my dear friend and music mentor, Sheila. Her soothing voice on the other end of the line was a lifeline. 'What's it like?' she asked, sensing my apprehension. I replied, 'There's cameras everywhere, Sheila.' She chuckled and gave me sage advice, 'Look for the red light on top of the camera, that means it's live. Sing your heart out, and look directly into it.'

Her words were a guiding star in the sea of nerves. As I walked back inside the TV studio, I spotted a red light on a camera. With Sheila's wisdom echoing in my mind, I stepped onto the stage, took a deep breath, and sang my heart out, knowing that this was a moment to cherish, even with the nerves and the millions of eyes watching.

It was a performance I would never forget, a beautiful blend of fear and excitement, and it marked a milestone in my musical journey.

After that, the success kept on going. Our music became

very popular in Scandinavian countries (Sweden, Denmark and Norway) and the rest of Europe. Wherever we went on stage, people in the crowd would be chanting, "Super MAXX, Super MAXX!"

During an unforgettable 10-day tour in Toronto, Canada, I found myself singing on a big revolving stage. But in the midst of the act, I had an unexpected guest – a mosquito had landed on my tongue as I was singing with my mouth open, adding a surprising twist to my performance. Naturally, I had no choice but to gulp it down mid-song, but I couldn't help but feel sad for the innocent mosquito. It clearly didn't want to go that way.

On one occasion, I found myself caught in a whirlwind of 15 back-to-back radio and magazine interviews - all in one day! and while the opportunity was incredible, the sheer exhaustion made it less fun. As a young adult, I felt I did not know how to fully express the way I was feeling, as journalist after journalist would ask the same questions: 'How did it all begin?', 'Who inspires you?', 'What City do you love to perform in best?', 'When is the next single out?', and on and on and on it went.

Looking back at those days, I would often find myself wishing for the support of a wise and experienced mentor by my side. Someone who could have provided valuable insights, shared their wealth of knowledge, and offered guidance when navigating the complex terrain of the music world. I yearned for a sense of security in a music industry filled with cut-throat competition and numerous pitfalls.

One day, an unexpected phone call from the Daily Mail, a prominent UK newspaper, rang in my hotel room. They were keen to explore my journey to success, but they had a specific appetite for a captivating story. In their pursuit of an attention-grabbing narrative, they asked about whether I had ever had any stalkers. My response, however, was a resounding "no."

Undeterred, they were determined to craft a meaningful feature for their readers. The journalistic imagination kicked into high gear, and they came up with an intriguing twist: a heartwarming tale of a welcome home banner. According to the newspaper, the military and their families back home had gone above and beyond during my last homecoming after an extensive touring stint. They had placed a massive, heartfelt welcome home banner outside my house.

But the embellishment didn't end there. The Daily Mail's creative flair continued with a fictional story about my "lucky socks." According to their narrative, I had a quirky travel ritual, without which no journey was complete. These supposedly enchanted socks had become a talisman of sorts, a source of comfort and good fortune on every gig-bound adventure.

This small written piece in the newspaper marked a chapter in my music career, demonstrating the power of storytelling in the world of entertainment and journalism, but it also showed me that they could make things up, and that scared me.

In the entertainment business, the mantra 'sex sells' often prevails. As a sensitive soul in the music industry, I grappled not only with the harsh demands of the business but also with my own body image issues and a profound lack of self-love. It was a challenging combination that required inner strength, and I often questioned how I managed to not just survive, but also stay true to myself.

It was inevitable that burnout would catch up with me, and when it finally did, it was a bolt out of the blue.

The fourth digital healing tone is 417 Hz, is based at the sacral energy centre, and is all about 'Facilitating Change.' This tone is about embracing new beginnings with ease and grace, helping you to break free from old habits and patterns. Supports emotional healing, especially related to past traumas and unresolved issues.

Reflect: Think about some of the ways in which you can actively embrace change and bring in new beginnings. What old habits do you need to let go of? Are there any past traumas or unresolved issues you need to let go of?

Use the space here to write (or in your journal) about a time when everything went right for you. What were the events that led up to this? How were you living in your flow? What thoughts, ideas and insights came up for you while reading this chapter?

_____

_____

_____

_____

_____

_____

_____

_____

Vintage Elegance: MAXX First Photoshoot in Berlin, Germany, 1994

Press Spotlight: Capturing The Moment In A Newspaper Photo

5

BURNOUT & THE MEDICAL CLAIM!

We toured constantly throughout '94 and '95. At first, it was exhilarating. But it soon became exhausting – I was completely worn out.

"No more, no more I can't stand it,
No more, no more
No more, no more I can't stand it,
No more, no more
He said: I'm gonna take you high,
Gonna take you low
Gonna take you everywhere I go
Gonna take you high
Gonna take you low
But I can't stand it, no, no more
No, no more."

Singing those lyrics three to four times a week felt very normal to me. It was like the words were made for the truth of how I was feeling inside.

At the time, I couldn't fully grasp the depth of what I was going through, but it was an experience of total burnout. The relentless demands of the music industry, the constant touring, and the overall pressure had taken a toll on my physical and emotional well-being. The exhaustion I felt was not just the result of a few late nights; it was a fatigue that went to the very core of my being.

Every day became a battle against weariness, as I struggled to find the energy to perform, engage in interviews, and meet the expectations placed upon me. The relentless pace left me feeling like a shadow of my former self, drained and depleted. Burnout wasn't just about feeling tired; it was about feeling utterly and completely spent as if there was nothing left to give. I was constantly on the road, in chauffeur-driven limousines and flying around from airport to airport, sleeping in five-star hotels, eating between long periods of sleep, performances on TV, radio and big music festivals, VIP meet and greets with fans, professional photoshoots and performing in music videos. It felt like a half-existence.

One day in Amsterdam, after working some shows, I woke up in my hotel room with my whole face and head covered in eczema and psoriasis. I was sore and red all around my eyes, ears and scalp. It was nowhere else on my body, just my face, and in my hair. I was in a lot of pain and felt terrible. I can only describe it as a burning sensation and very inflamed. So, I phoned the tour manager and told him that I was unable to do the photoshoot booked for that day, and he asked to see me. He turned up at my hotel room door and was shocked. He cancelled the shoot right away.

It was after this that I decided to take stock of my life, reflecting on the countless hours spent with different makeup and hair products. The constant whirlwind of flying on planes four or five times a week, often far from home, had me yearning for the comforting presence of my two beloved cats. Stressful, intense interviews, back-to-back stage performances, and the relentless pace of the music industry had taken their toll on my well-being. This moment of introspection served as a turning point, prompting me to re-evaluate my priorities and seek a more balanced and fulfilling personal and professional life.

When I arrived back in the UK, I decided to seek help for my persistent skin conditions. These ailments had been a constant source of discomfort and frustration; despite consulting with multiple professional and private doctors spending an absolute fortune, no remedy seemed to provide relief. Until one day, after visiting five different doctors in a week, I reached out to an old friend, as I recalled her daughter's struggle with severe eczema during childhood.

Desperate for a solution, I phoned and asked about the treatment that had helped her daughter. Her response was simple yet life-changing: 'Baby shampoo and Vaseline.' It was a remedy I had never considered before. So, each night, I washed my hair with gentle baby shampoo and then generously applied Vaseline all over my face. This combination turned out to be a soothing balm for the relentless redness and pain that had troubled me for so long. The relief was like a breath of fresh air in my ongoing battle with these skin conditions, and it took me another two years to finally heal.

I found out sometime later that MAXX was due to go to the US, but sadly, it didn't happen because the management team thought we weren't committed enough. It wasn't that; it was an industry working us too hard, and me not really appreciating that my 24-year-old body couldn't handle this huge amount of stress. I think if they had taken the time out to speak with me directly on this, it would have been agreed to have some down time and return to touring again soon.

But sadly, that didn't happen.

Soon afterward, my management phoned me at home to ask how I was doing, and they mentioned that we were still the most likeable group on their roster to date, as they were still receiving large postal bags full of fan mail. I so would have liked to have replied back to all those fan letters. It would have probably cheered me up. Looking back, I just needed some good rest and some direct dialogue with some fans. I probably just needed to feel appreciated again and not like a puppet being played by a music industry that didn't ask me what my needs were. You hear these stories many times from other artists; it's very common. By 1996, MAXX was over.

From 1998-1999, after a two-year break, I joined a local

girl trio group, and we toured the UK and Germany singing cover songs, but I felt that after the high life and fame I had previously experienced in MAXX, it just wasn't the same. I missed being in the spotlight and craved to get back onto the big stage and do it all again, but I knew it wasn't that easy. The other two girls were so different to me. While I craved a soothing cup of hot milky tea after a gig and a wind-down, they preferred alcohol and partying. The moment I decided to part ways, though, our differences turned our working relationship into a wild brawl invitation. I gracefully declined the fight, but I can tell you that was the day I realised I was well and truly done with the music business.

The incident was a striking example of the challenges that can arise in the music industry, particularly the less glamorous side that's often hidden from public view. It illuminated the jealousy and competition that can simmer just beneath the surface, even among those who, at first, seem like allies.

Jealousy among singers, while not universal, is not uncommon. It's an industry where success can be fleeting, and the pressure to stay relevant is unrelenting. The achievements of one artist can sometimes cast a shadow of insecurity over others, leading to strained relationships and even open hostility. The incident with these two former girl group members reminded me that navigating this world required a thick skin and a resilient spirit, as well as a strong commitment to staying true to oneself.

Also, I would like to add that the entertainment industry,

like many others, is not immune to the dynamics of power and gender. It's not uncommon for men to make advances toward their female counterparts (and vice versa), and when those advances are declined, the aftermath can be challenging. In some cases, rejection can lead to a sudden change in attitude, where once-friendly colleagues might begin to ignore you or even make your professional life difficult. This, among other reasons, became a significant factor in my decision to step away from the industry for a while, as I had experienced this myself. And all of this left a nasty taste in my mouth. I was done.

In 1999, I bought my first house in South Manchester, a stone's throw from where I'd grown up. I was longing for some peace, grounding, and a secure foundation. Except, Shop and Grill café was now gone – instead, it had transformed into Linda's Pantry on Ducie Street in Manchester Town Centre near Piccadilly Train Station. My mother had switched premises, and the Pantry was a huge hit – there were often queues out the front cafe door as the Piccadilly area was getting a completely new renovation, a big project over a few years, with new apartments and a five-star hotel so that many builders would flock there for their breakfast and lunch breaks. I decided to take on more responsibility and spent most of my days working in the cafe. I missed singing and performing, though.

In 2000, I got the opportunity to move to Naples, Italy. I ended up working as a civilian secretary for the British

Military on a NATO camp, and I was also doing the odd solo gigs, but nothing much. At one point, I even had all my own musical equipment shipped over - mixing desk, speakers, and microphone costing me a couple of hundred pounds!

I came back to the UK around 2003, and something inside my heart and soul, did not ever want to sing again. I had no desire, and I could only explain it as 'a fire had died inside of me,' so I made a decision to study personal development, hoping that this may unlock my singing voice and help raise my self-confidence. I became certified in NLP (neurolinguistic programming), EFT (emotional freedom technique), and many more healing modalities. I was a workshop junkie! Most weekends, you would find me in some sort of training, and although I loved it, my singing voice still did not want to reappear. It just didn't feel safe enough yet, and I wondered if it ever would again. So I continued learning and studying, determined to solve this riddle.

In 2004, I moved to London to work as a make-up consultant for a famous beauty company. Completely random, I know, but it had always been an interest of mine because I had achieved great art grades back in my school days. It seemed the most natural transition to take. They soon trained me, and I started working at Fenwick's of New Bond Street and then eventually moved onto their main beauty counter at Harrods in Knightsbridge. Sometimes, private Chauffeurs would park at one of the side entry doors late at night, and I, and some of my other work colleagues on the other beauty counters, would be asked to put together the latest and most expensive make-up products in a gift box for a special famous VIP –we were never told who it was for, but it was a lot of fun working there, at least for a time.

I did that for 12 months, then moved back up north to Manchester, my self-confidence now at an all-time low. I was looking to fully nurture myself and find peace in my heart. My past musical experiences I think, had made me internalise and suppress my deepest feelings, and I was struggling to let them out in a safe and trusted environment. I needed to know how to release and let go with ease, but I always seemed to be working, busy on the go, doing something, and not truly being.

Whenever I did go to sing – in the shower, the car, or even my own music room, wherever – I could only get a few notes out. My throat felt tight like it could not say what it really wanted to say. It was just the tip of the iceberg. I was in a miserable headspace, and more bad things were heading my way.

In the spring of 2007, when I was 38, something pivotal happened in my life. I went to my local dentist's surgery to have all my mercury fillings replaced with white resin. As a singer, I wanted to be more aesthetically pleasing when I opened my mouth! There was a lot of work to do, and I had a three-hour appointment booked one Saturday afternoon.

I opened my mouth, and the dentist began his work. But an hour into treatment, whilst working on the top left-hand corner of my mouth, the small diamond burr fell off the electric drill and fell onto the back of my tongue. I couldn't flick it out and, reflexively, I gulped and swallowed the small instrument. The dentist put his hand on my right shoulder as I turned around and stared at him in complete shock, because for a moment, I thought I was literally going to die. The tiny razor-sharp burr was working its way down my throat and through my internal system. It could be causing all kinds of unknown damage to my insides, I thought, so I quickly asked the dental nurse where the kitchen was, and I ran towards it, grabbed a pint glass from the cupboard, and kept filling water from the tap quickly gulping it to try and flush it out of my body. I have never drunk water so fast in my life! I then drove myself to the nearest hospital for investigations and a long claim ensued. I was passed from pillar to post with doctors and psychologists advising me not to continue with the medical negligence claim. This dental mishap solidified my low confidence even more in singing, and my voice eventually dried up. My throat would ache, and my heart would beat faster, and I firmly believed that I would never sing again. And I developed a phobia of dentists.

I took a significant step toward justice by hiring a medical negligence solicitor to pursue a claim regarding the dental drill bur incident. However, fate had an ironic twist in store. The female solicitor I chose was pregnant at the time, and as her labor got closer, she was unable to dedicate the attention my case required. Consequently, she passed my case down to her young assistant, who, to my dismay, proved to be less than effective.

At the outset, the solicitor had offered assurance, stating that I had a strong chance of winning the case. When I was only six months from the deadline to file my claim, which was set at three years, the solicitor dropped a bombshell. In a letter, she informed me that they would no longer continue with my case, citing doubts about its potential for success. To add insult to injury, an invoice for £7,000 arrived, leaving me utterly flabbergasted.

This abrupt about-face in legal representation was a bitter pill to swallow, leaving me not only emotionally drained but also financially burdened. It was a stark reminder of the challenges one could face while seeking justice in a system that often felt stacked against the individual.

In the face of the disheartening setback with my previous solicitor, I was determined not to let my quest for justice be forgotten. With a mere six months left to file my claim in court, I began to search for a new solicitor who would be willing to take on my case at such short notice. The pursuit led me to a dedicated solicitor in Birkenhead, a distance of 40 miles from my home.

Over the course of the next four years, this tenacious legal professional took on the challenge of my medical negligence case. It was a remarkable journey, as winning medical claims is often regarded as a daunting, uphill battle. I was just so fed up with the injustice in the world that I decided to be brave and go for it. I'm so pleased I did, as seven years later, I won an out-of-court settlement and was one of a few people who ever won against the medical profession.

But who would have known that this whole dental accident would force me to make a big life-changing decision a few years later?

In late December 2007, while on holiday in Murcia, Spain celebrating Christmas with some family members, it seemed that the dental accident was making me reflect back on my life. I have to be completely honest here with you, my life had been tested by many a close relationships since being a teenager. I seemed to have dated males with all kinds of addictions, from alcohol, drugs, womanising, smoking, to gambling, the lot, I'd seen and suffered it all. The dental accident really was a catalyst for me waking up to me, and not tolerating anyone else's problems, but focusing on clearing my own stuff and loving myself.

I secretly wished to share my life with someone special, I wanted to have some good luck and be put on the right path. I wrote a secret wish list on a piece of paper, of the person I would really like to spend my life with, and then performed that same ritual that I used before I went on stage to sing, all those many years ago.

Standing on the Spanish villa balcony, with the warm nightly air blowing around me, I put my hands up to the starry sky, and said, "God, please don't send me any more crap!".

And I asked, "If there is someone out there who is meant to be with me in this lifetime, then so be it, but if there is no one special, then I prefer to remain single for the rest of my days because It has to be right". " I won't settle for anything less." "I would like to share my life with someone who is meant for me, and me for them. That's it, thank you". I had hope. And dreams. It had worked once before, like I said, when I was at the singing talent competition all those years ago at the military camp in Germany back in 1993. Maybe it could work again? Maybe? Whoever came into my life next had to be better than what had come before.

Linda's Pantry: My Mum's Second Cafe on Ducie Street, Manchester

The fifth digital healing tone is 528 Hz, is based at the solar plexus energy centre and is all about "'Transformation and Miracles.' This tone is also believed to support DNA repair (although more studies are needed to be done on this).

Reflect: How do you transform your life for the better? What miracles have you experienced so far in your life? Imagine your personal DNA strong and active and in optimum working order. What would that look, feel and sound like?

Use the space here to write (or in your journal) about a time when you wished, prayed or asked for something better in your life. What happened? How did it appear? What thoughts, ideas and insights came up for you while reading this chapter?

_____
_____
_____
_____
_____
_____
_____
_____
_____
_____

Solo Photoshoot In The Late 90's

6

THE VISION & THE WEDDING!

After the dental incident, I had reached my lowest point. I was going through some dark nights of the soul, as I was back working long, busy days again in the café, setting my alarm for 5.30 a.m. to get showered and dressed, then driving to work to open the doors for 6.30 a.m. I had also taken on a new music course to become a qualified vocal teacher, at the local music college a few streets away in town, and I had also been offered a new part-time job teaching students music performance at the same college. That same tiredness was affecting me again, I was doing too much. I felt so disillusioned and just needed some rest.

Then one day in January 2008, while driving home from work, my mind suddenly flashed to what I can only describe as a 'vision' of a football team dressing room, with a long L-shaped wooden bench, and rows of royal blue coloured football shirts with big white numbers on the back hanging on coat hooks. I then saw the back of someone's head with short dark hair, delivering EFT (Emotional Freedom Technique) to all the footballers sitting on the benches.

I said, 'What's this?', 'This isn't me or my future. I'm not delivering EFT to footballers,' 'I'm a singer"

Then, all of a sudden, the vision disappeared quickly as it had come, and I was back in my own head, driving down the road in my car.

What was that? Where had it come from? I might have been scared, but I took it as a positive sign. Something good was on its way to me.

And it happened sooner than I thought.

The following day, a regular customer came into the café. I hadn't seen this person for a long time, and he would normally in the past come in, order a breakfast sandwich and a cup of tea, and after a brief chat with me about healing techniques like reiki and personal development courses, he would leave.

But this day was different. He came in, ordered his usual meal to eat in, and sat down at one of the cafe tables. I had known him for a long time and he had never once done this before.

I found myself sat opposite him, in between the many jobs I had to do in the cafe, and we got talking about Reiki together – a welcome change from the usual, everyday cafe chat!

He said there was going to be a Reiki night at his friend's house in two nights' time, and he asked if I wanted to come along to it. I said no, because I was so busy with getting up early to work in the cafe, all the music homework for my course I had to do, and also the students I was teaching, a few times a week, I would not be able to make it.

But there was something really strange happening. Each time I stood up to leave the table and go back into the kitchen, I would be drawn back again to where he was sat, three times it happened.

At the final moment, I sat there and asked with wonder, "So who will be at this reiki night then?" He replied, "Well, there will be the lady whose house it is being held at, her daughter, her best friend, and David. He delivers EFT to a football team!

I thought, 'I best go'. It was a sign, from what I had seen in my vision two days previous.

So on Thursday, 17th January 2008, I went to the Reiki night. And that is where I met David. The love of my life.

The first time I met him, he gave me a big, warm hug and a beautiful smile. It was the best hug I have ever experienced in my life. The best ever!

He was 42, and I was 38. We hit it off immediately, talking pretty much non-stop as if no one else in the room existed. We both knew that this was a divine meeting of souls; he has told me since that he knew from the moment he first met me that he had to marry me.

The world works in mysterious ways – and I'm so glad it does!

It was now early February, and it took David nearly three whole weeks to ask me out for a date. He had never had to ask anyone out on a date before in all his 42 years, because of his funny sense of humour, women would ask him out for a date, so this was the first time when he met me, he knew he would have to pluck up the courage, and he also knew we would get married.

I believe it had to be this way, that it was set up that he had to ask me. I certainly wasn't going to ask any man out on a date, I was honouring my traditional values, since all my past relationships had failed miserably. I was not normally a good judge of character, I always took people at face value and trusted they were good souls, when they were not, so this time I knew it had to be different. He had to ask me out, which thankfully he did.

Our first date day arrived, Wednesday 6th February 2008, 21 days after we had first met. He tells me he was so nervous that it took him those three weeks to pick up the courage to ask me out on a date.

We had agreed to meet in a coffee shop in St.Annes Square, and I remember I was so tired after an early start opening the cafe, and also attending college that as I turned the corner to walk towards the coffee shop, I said to myself 'I'll only be an hour' as I knew I had to be up early again for work the following day.

Nine hours later, we were still out on our first date! We shared stories and laughed together over our peppermint herbal teas, we walked onto the Oriental Chinese Buffet and ate a lovely 'all you can eat' menu, drove in his car to a popular crystal shop in Ashton-under-Lyne where we looked at the many gemstones, jewellery, ornaments and other items.

We then drove 20 miles to Hollingworth Lake in Littleborough and stayed until dark, walking halfway around the lake, we hugged a big tree and talked with a tawny owl up above, that hooted nearby. We talked and laughed a lot, and it was the best date of my life. We regularly go back to Hollingworth Lake now, often to mark our anniversary.

Two nights later, we had our second date, where we parked up at Sale Water Park, sharing a bag of chips from the local chip shop. Talking and laughing again, it felt so natural and normal.

On 21st May 2008, four months and four days after our first meeting, we were married in Cusco, Peru by a Shaman called 'Francisco'. We were the first western couple to get married by the Willoq community, who had Inca heritage and spoke the Quechua language.

We found out that we had both read the book - 'The Celestine Prophecy' by James Redfield about 20 years previously, which is about a main character who goes on an adventure to find and understand a series of nine spiritual insights in an ancient manuscript in Peru and has a spiritual awakening, as he then goes through a transitional period in his life.

So our choice to get married in Peru, was a perfect decision for us, as we both loved the book and the story attached to it.

Our marriage took place over ten hours in three archaeological sites. Moray, Chinchero and the Sacred

Valley. We wore traditional Willoq wedding outfits, with multi-coloured ponchos and hats with real fresh flowers in. In the lead-up to our journey to Peru, we had sent over measurements for our wedding headwear. However, there was a mix-up with our hat sizes. To our surprise, my hat was too big, causing it to wobble and slide down the back of my head. And David's hat had the opposite issue, hugging his head too tightly, making his face all squashed up.

Francisco and his wife had hand-carved two metal wedding rings and silver and white bracelets. My ring, is in the shape of the figure of eight, infinity symbol and David's ring has three carved Inca symbols. The ceremony was followed by a vibrant feast, showcasing the rich flavours of Peruvian cuisine. They had a unique tradition of preparing a ceremonial underground oven, which is called the 'Pachamanca.' This intricate process involved digging a pit in the earth and heating it for 24 hours before creating the perfect conditions for slow-cooking meats and potatoes. We drank drinks such as 'Pisco Sour,' a cocktail featuring Pisco, a grape brandy, blended with zesty lime juice, sugar, and frothy egg white, and 'Chicha Morada,' a sweet purple corn drink infused with spices. There was a live band, with one musician playing a wind instrument called the Conch Shell, which is a huge sea shell. We danced all night long, swinging each other around and created some beautiful memories.

While exploring the small, close-knit village of the Willoq community, we stumbled upon a heartwarming treasure

- beautifully handcrafted blankets adorned with bright Peruvian colours. These blankets weren't just pieces of fabric; they were woven tapestries of culture and tradition. One particular blanket stood out, and we knew instantly that it was more than just a keepsake. It was a wonderful reminder of our wedding day, a day filled with love, fun, and the promise of a very happy and prosperous future together.

We do believe as a couple, we are very powerful together, and we know that we have come here to be part of the great awakening, to ascend and help others.

Between 2008-11, since becoming fully qualified with a music teaching diploma, I was lucky to be involved with a UK government-funded programme that would help to reinstate singing in all primary schools by 2012 in England, called 'Sing Up' - all in good time for the London Olympic Games 2012.

Working as a Freelance Vocal Coach, my hours were flexible, and I had about five different coaching roles in all that I would drive to each week. One day I would be working at a primary school with teachers, the next day I would be working with young mums and their babies, and on one particular job which I found very interesting, I would teach young adults with mental health challenges (some would even have their own carers with them) - a two hour creative workshop (one hour of singing and one hour of poem creative writing), it was great fun. Each week I would photocopy the song lyrics of the songs I had chosen a few days before onto an A4 piece of paper, so everyone had a ' handout', and we would all sing along together to the backing music.

One day, I printed the lyrics out to an old 1970s classic song "I Can See Clearly Now' written and recorded by American singer-songwriter Johnny Nash.

Once we'd sang the song, I noticed something unusual happen within the group, because I am NLP trained, I notice body language and emotional state changes, and one particular woman was shaking all over, as her whole body rocked forward so fast and positively with a big smile on her face, as she said out loud 'Can we do it again, Can we do it again?' I was shocked. So we sang the whole song again, and again, and again, three more times, the whole group was rocking, shaking, moving, jumping and dancing literally around the room in our big circle, as they raised their voices, sang from their hearts with big cheesy grins all over their faces!

> *I can see clearly now the rain has gone*
> *I can see all the obstacles in my way*
> *Gone are the dark clouds that had me blind*
> *It's gonna be a bright (bright) bright sunshiny day*
> *It's gonna be a bright (bright) bright sunshiny day*
> *Oh, yes I can make it now the pain has gone*
> *All of the bad feelings have disappeared*
> *Here is that rainbow I've been praying for*
> *It's gonna be a bright (bright) bright sunshiny day*

All that positivity in the room had inspired me. I had been working with this particular group for about six months and had never witnessed this before. This really set me thinking.

When I got home afterwards, I went straight into my music room, turned on my music PA equipment, and pressed play. I began to sing 'Dreams' by The Corrs. I managed to sing the first verse, then it got to the chorus, and my critical mind started to say to me, 'No, you're no good, stop now' - so I did.

It was common for me to sing the first verse, and then not even get to the chorus. It had been this way for a while, since the late 90s really, and although I was used to it by now, I felt it was more a mental and emotional block on my part, and I wanted it to be gone. I stood in the middle of my music room, and although this time I didn't look at the night sky (it was daytime), I raised my hands up into the air and said, 'God if you're listening, I really want to sing again. I know I have come here to do good in this world, so please come through me, teach me what it is I have to do, so I can sing again'.

I wouldn't say I was religious at all, more spiritual, although I did attend catholic schools growing up, and to be honest, I never did fully embrace it and take it on as my truth. I'm not really anything, but I do believe there is a God, a source, a creator, an energy, good and whole.

I thought about what had happened in the day within the singing group and the Johnny Nash song. How everyone seemed so happy and free, with big smiles across their faces.

I wondered why most (not all) music to date was so

lyrically aggressive, negative and over-sexualised. Remember I've been songwriting since I was a teenager about lost love, looking for love, abandoned love, so when I realised that 'words really matter,' my head was blown! Why hadn't I thought of this earlier? What would it be like for all songs on the planet to have positive uplifting lyrics in their songs? What would that do to us as a species and for the world? I then received again what I can only explain as another vision, similar to what had happened to me while driving home from the cafe that day with the person delivering EFT to a football team in my mind's eye, but this time it was auditory. I could hear it. And it repeated three times, clearly into my right ear.

The words said, 'There is going to be an energy, a love energy filtering down onto the Earth in the near future, and it will change the planet for good with a positive love vibration and create a higher frequency' - I couldn't believe my ears. What was this? I felt excited and nervous. What would be my role in this I thought?

I asked again, "God, I know I have come here to do good. Please come through me and use me to spread this message of love in music from now on. I will write and sing the new songs, and I will do your work. Thank you'. I then saw our beautiful planet surrounded by an energetic grid of positive energy, full of love. It was going to be sent down to heal the planet for good.

This is awesome, I thought, how cool! A new energy was going to come to the planet, and it was called 'the love energy'.

It was then I decided that I would write my first solo album titled 'The Love Energy' and that this would be a very special piece of work.

I couldn't believe it! This download was a game-changer. I realised then that I was going to have to work with positive lyrics from now on, and that I was going to make a huge difference in the world and share this mysterious love energy. And eventually I would create a new music industry, one based on love and positivity. My voice and my songs had the power to make the world a better place. I knew it, I just needed to find it again and start writing.

Literally, the very next day, I was driving down the road and immediately started to receive a full down-load of positive lyrics that would later appear on the album. The words just flowed into me. While I still wasn't fully comfortable singing, I knew that this was a huge step in the right direction.

The Love Energy, will set me free
Is Lifting me right now
The Love Energy, is lifting me
Will set me Free right now
Love, Love, Energy is lifting me

Soon after this download, more continued to come, and I had managed to write three positive songs with full lyrics in a week, ' Just Be Yourself', ' Blessed with Love' and 'The Love Energy (Part I).

Then one day I was browsing on the internet and came across a question that someone was asking; 'Why does the Music Industry use 440 Hz vibration as its Standard Concert Pitch for all music and musical instruments around the world'?

When I looked further into it, it was said that it makes us all feel and think the same and that it had been set to manipulate and control the masses, as I mentioned in the beginning of this book.

I then learnt that 528 Hz - called 'The Love Frequency' by Dr Len Horowitz was the correct frequency and that all music should be tuned to, and not 440. I also discovered 432 Hz, which is powerful too! This new information I was discovering on the many different digital tones opened up my mind even further, and I couldn't wait to begin my album.

I found myself asking, 'What if I write positive lyrics in all of my songs, and then 'tune' them to a different hertz frequency - could this really help shift the planet and raise its vibration? Could this change in music really bring 'The Love Energy' into existence, and help clean and heal the planet for good?

Lately, I've heard some people talk about a new energy that is coming down to the planet, and it's called 'The Love Wave,' which I feel is very similar to the words and vibration of 'The Love Energy,' so it's all very exciting!

Somehow, in the haze of all the negative worded songs out there, I could see that my love energy music could cut through the gloom and truly lighten up the world. I was filled with excitement, and it made me want to do something to change the current system right away. I decided to take a leap and dedicate myself to something radical. Something that would stop the negativity of the establishment, the current music industry, from winning. I thought if I'm unable to sing right now, for whatever reason, then I will start again from scratch'.'I will let go, release all of my lower emotional blockages, and all of my negative thought patterns, and I'll just go for it.' 'I'll start again.' So I did.

On 25th July 2012, I sold my house, my car, gave away all my material possessions and cleared out. I put some small pieces into storage, and told my second solicitor who took on my medical claim, that I would be gone for a while. The first solicitor was actually taking me to court (the cheek of it, after what I had endured), and I also thought to myself, 'Well if I haven't got anything, then they won't win or take my house from me, will they?' So with my second solicitor fully backing me, I set off with David, for a once in a lifetime world trip adventure and most importantly find my singing voice again!

The sixth digital healing tone is 639 Hz, is based at the heart energy centre, and is all about 'Reconnecting and Balancing Relationships'. This tone is used as a harmonious bridge in opening up and healing our hearts.

Reflect: How do you connect and open your heart? What do you need to do right now to receive and give love from your beautiful heart?

Use the space here to write (or in your journal) about a time you have followed your heart. What were the positive things that came from it? What needs to happen to heal and open your heart? What thoughts, ideas and insights came up for you while reading this chapter?

_____
_____
_____
_____
_____
_____
_____
_____
_____
_____

David and me on our special Wedding Day with the Willoq Community, Peru - 21st May 2008

David and me at The Rotary Club, Birkenhead 2012

7

NEPAL & FINDING MY VOICE AGAIN!

With the freedom of selling all my worldly goods, letting go of the constant worry of the legal claim, and all the downloads I had received about love energy, I was on top of the world. The revelations I had had about the music industry really challenged my belief system and I wasn't even sure if I would ever get to sing again. I thought about the negative music, and how when I first finished in the industry back in the 90s I was told by my then manager, 'sex sells.' I felt like a failure. I felt that you had to be sexy to be famous, and it wasn't at all about the voice or the talent, but the image and how much skin you were willing to expose to the world. I wondered about the first few tracks of The Love Energy Album, sitting on my computer at home, the positivity behind each song.

David and I arrived in Nepal in 2012 to begin our voluntary work. With the house sold, we didn't have a fixed base, so we could go anywhere we wanted!

We decided to work in a Buddhist Monastery, David would teach English and I, of course, would teach music. But when we arrived at this particular monastery, it soon became clear that the elders were not all what they seemed. There are many Monasteries in Nepal, and each one so very different. It all depends on who is in charge and what money they make.

After spending a week in a local hostel and some sightseeing, we got a taxi to take us to our new work place. The Rinpoche – the chosen head of the Monastery – was sitting on a small wooden chair in the main grounds whilst a young boy was massaging his bald head, surrounded by another group of young boys. He gave us the biggest smile, with eyes beaming and bright. Behind, a circle of young adult monks were chanting and performing their daily Tai Chi classes, but David – with his strong empathic abilities – instantly saw straight through them, observing that they were more distracted by the new Westerners arriving, instead of being entirely focused on their practice as we walked in through the gates past the front where they all were.

The Monastery itself was disgustingly dirty, and so as soon as we had dropped our luggage off in our room, and had a briefing with the head monk on what our duties were (starting at 5.30 a.m. the very next morning) we headed straight down the road to the local hardware shop and bought a brush, mop, bucket and cleaning products. We spent the rest of the afternoon cleaning, and making our room as homely as we could. But in the middle of the night, we were woken by an infestation of cockroaches, and there were so many other problems there, with Elders sneaking down the road to the fancy restaurant to eat, whilst we would wait in a queue with the other monks, young adults and children, to be fed a plate of rice and vegetables.

Waking up at 5.00 a.m. again on the second day, after only one day of teaching we had surprisingly found the monks to be undisciplined and mischievous. The flask of hot water they had provided us the night before was now cold, and there were no lights working in the bathroom for us to see properly to have a wash and for David to shave.

We decided to pack our bags. We had lasted two days. The Voluntary Organisation moved us to the Kathmandu Valley, where we lived with a family of nine who had a cow and a buffalo. We taught at a local community school – I taught singing and sign language – just like I did back in Manchester with the young mums and babies. It was a simple and slow paced time, but rewarding. During weekends on our days off, we would hop on the overcrowded bus and head down the valley, into the main town to have lunch and walk around the shops.

Close to Christmas in December 2012, three of the children in the house put on a performance for us, playing instruments, dancing and singing. It was so sweet and wonderful. It brought tears to my eyes! I still wasn't able to sing myself at this point but the head of the house turned around and said to us, "Your turn." David said, "Elyse is the singer of the family." I was nervous; I hadn't sung in public for over 10 years at that point. But now, in this restful place in the valley, with thousands of stars twinkling bright in the dark sky above, I ended up singing 'Love Energy' and 'Blessed with Love' – which both appear on the album. They loved it! The host said that although he didn't understand what I had sung (he didn't speak English so the children would translate for him) he said my vocal tone was fantastic and he thanked me.

The following day in school, a huge group of children ran up to me and shouted 'Miss, Miss was that you singing in the valley last night?" Unbeknown to me, my voice had travelled all around the valley to the locals, and they all heard me sing. My singing had gone far and wide. In the Kathmandu Valley, sound really carries!

Singing the evening before had unblocked my throat energy centre from the accident. My voice finally felt free!

Unfortunately, very soon after, I got food poisoning, which is very common in Nepal. I spent a couple of days in hospital, and we booked a four-star hotel for me to rest and recover. Then, thankfully some very good news arrived, after five years, all the stress and sacrifices paid off - I had won the claim.

With my determination, belief and renewed sense of hope, I had beaten the odds of winning a case against the medical profession. I had done it!

As soon as I was recovered and out of the hospital, I decided that I was going to go home and create my album.

Flying from Nepal in January 2013, back home to a cold, wet rainy England, one of the first things I did was contact my local recording studio to book a full-day session. I felt ready to lay down my vocals for my new forthcoming album, 'The

Love Energy,' and to talk with the Producer about 'tuning' the album to 528 Hz. The Producer said he had never heard of 'tuning' songs to a different frequency before, but he would research it and see what he could do to make it happen.

Soon afterward, I was visiting the Stockport Mind Body Spirit (MBS) Event one Saturday afternoon, and I got talking to the organiser. I mentioned that I was creating my first solo album, and she said, 'Great, can you sing here tomorrow?' - she really put me on the spot. I hesitated at first, as it had been a long time since I had performed in public (aside from in front of the Nepal host family and the rest of the Kathmandu Valley, of course!). But I knew I really needed to push myself, step out of my comfort zone, and make a full commitment to this kind offer, so I said yes.

The very next day, I rocked up with my CD player, a microphone and a speaker. I found a small table and a plug socket at the back of the room and propped myself up. There were some nearby stallholders selling crystals, hand-made jewellery, and spiritual books, and as I began to sing a few of my new album tracks, they were really well received, and I gained some nice smiles and made some new contacts.

I remembered that every time I had tried to sing a song in the more recent past, I could only sing a few bars, and then I would stop and give up. So putting myself under this pressure and singing my new songs at this event was interesting because I had a different feel about them, mainly because the lyrics were so positive. And it worked, as the event organiser asked me to sing again at the next event in a few months' time. I said yes!

The studio producer had done his research on being able to tune my album to 528 Hz, and was confident we could make it work. He knew it was a completely new concept and was up for trying something innovative. I was super excited!

After a few studio sessions, he asked one day when I was leaving the studio, 'How many songs will your album have?' I didn't have a clue. I had never thought of this before. I just knew I had written three songs so far, and that was it.

So, while driving home that day from the studio and completely forgetting the question I got asked, I kept hearing the word "nine" from the right-hand side of my head, in my right ear. 'Nine,' I replied out loud, 'What does that mean? I replied to the strange voice that kept repeating quietly and softly, 'nine,' 'nine,' 'nine.' I got annoyed at one point, as I didn't understand, so eventually, I said, "OK! Nine it is!" Not knowing the full reason why.

In between recording album tracks at the studio, I would eventually go on to tour most of the MBS events across the northwest of England, also driving down south to London, and even further up north to Scotland. I was having a great time on my mini-tour of the UK. I would speak to people at my own stall, sing live on stage, and hold musical frequency workshops in the side rooms, which went down really well, and then people would sign up to join my email newsletter list.

To be honest, when people first listened to my songs back then, it seemed they just weren't used to this type of positive lyrical pop music; they thought it was happy-clappy or 'God's music' — they didn't get it. It just showed how much the current music industry is ingrained in us, where happy music with positive lyrics just isn't fully accepted yet because it's so rare. This was in 2013, and I noticed a dense energy in the air everywhere I went. People weren't waking up yet.

But I was.

The seventh digital healing tone is 741 Hz, is based at the throat energy centre, and is all about 'Clear Communication and Self-expression'. This tone enables you to resonate with speaking your truth and being authentic. It supports self-expression, allowing you to voice your thoughts and feelings with confidence. Helps release a good singing voice. Reflect: Imagine having clear, strong verbal communication, voicing your thoughts with truth and authenticity. What do you need to do right now to fully express yourself and speak with confidence with family, friends, work colleagues, children and animals?

Use the space here to write (or in your journal) about how you express yourself when you are living with a positive mindset and have a clear throat energy centre. How do you ask for things and share your truth with ease and joy? What thoughts, ideas and insights came up for you while reading this chapter?

_____

_____

_____

_____

_____

Capturing Solitude: A Striking Solo Photoshoot in 2014

On the Road in Style: Rocking My Dungarees Behind the Wheel in 2017!

8

A NEW NAME,
FINDING THE 9 TONES!

One day in 2013, I was contacted by a UK Booking Agent in London, asking me if I would like to reform MAXX. He asked If I could speak to the original rapper in Germany, and get the rights to the band name and backing tracks from the licence holders. I said I would try, as it had been a long time since I had spoken to everybody.

I found an old contact number for one of the main songwriters in Berlin and messaged him. We had a chat, and he told he would speak with the rapper and get back to me. And then nothing happened. I phoned and emailed a few times, and no answer. It was odd. A few months later I had a big surprise, the rapper was in Poland doing a MAXX show with a new girl singer!

I cried. Mainly because I was waiting around for those guys to contact me so that we could go out gigging together, but for some reason, they ignored my calls and emails, and then went out without me.

David said to me, 'Why are you crying, you are such a great singer songwriter, just continue to do your solo songs and it will be a huge success, the world needs love energy music.' I pulled myself together and agreed. He was right.

To mark this newfound start I decided to leave my old musical past behind and get myself a brand new artist name, because I knew that I would never be Linda from MAXX again.

BECOMING ELYSE

When I married David in Peru, back in 2008, I had become Linda Rogers, but I felt this name had a very country-and-western feel to it, and it just wasn't the stage name I was looking for. I do like country and Western music, but the musical style I sing is mainly pop and dance, so I had to find something more suitable and what felt right to me. And most importantly I was releasing a solo album called 'The Love Energy' so my current name had to change, but how and what would I choose? I hired a well-known name analyst and numerologist based in Manchester to look at my current name and give me some feedback to see if I should leave it as it is, or maybe consider changing my whole name. After a few weeks, he sent me a report suggesting that it would be best to change my name to something more unique and creative sounding, especially because it would be used for my solo music.

A few new name suggestions later, I chose the name Alyse, but when I collected the deed poll paperwork after work one day, it said 'Elyse'. There had been a slight typo mistake. So I took it as a sign and thought, 'Okay, that's my new name then'.

It felt right to me. I was a new woman entering the age of love energy with all my heart.

I have never looked back since August 2013 when I first officially changed my name, and I use this name in every area of my life now. I knew I was on the right path.

FINDING THE 9 TONES

One Sunday, I was attending a well-being event and I got talking with a nice couple about spiritual things. The event organiser came over to me while we were chatting and said, 'Elyse, would you like to sing at our next event?' I replied, 'Yes, of course that would be great.' So we agreed on a date, and as I turned back to speak to the couple, the man said, 'Sorry we overheard your conversation, did you say you were a singer?' I replied, "Yes I am, and I'm currently writing my first solo album which will be 'tuned' into 528 Hz frequency. His mouth opened wide in shock, and with his eyes surprised, he looked at his wife and then said to me, 'I'm looking for a singer. I'm a musician, and I've tuned my keyboard to different frequencies.' He continued, 'You do know that the 528 Hz frequency you mentioned, that there are eight more frequencies? I said, 'No, I didn't know that.' He said, "Yes, they are a set of nine tones, and they are called 'The Solfeggio

Frequencies.' I was happily shocked and excited, because here was the confirmation on why I kept hearing the number nine repeating in my head, that day whilst driving my car on the way home from the recording studio, it all made sense now. I decided then that The Love Energy Album would have nine tracks, and all of them would be 'tuned' to the different 9 Solfeggio frequencies and no longer just 528. It was perfect.

So, my journey with the 9 tones was an unexpected and profound discovery. As I explored the attributes of each tone, I realised the incredible depth and resonance they carried. From the transformative 528 Hz to the soothing 639 Hz, each tone had a unique purpose. It was as if I had uncovered a hidden treasure chest of healing frequencies.

To deepen my understanding and share this treasure trove of knowledge with others, I began integrating the tones into my music and healing practices. The results were nothing short of remarkable, with listeners reporting feelings of balance, clarity, and emotional release. I was not only mesmerised by the tones themselves but also by the incredible impact they had on those who experienced them.

At the MBS events I started my own study on the effects of the Solfeggio frequencies and how they actually worked.

During one event, I noticed that some of the stallholders were not very happy because the room was very quiet with no customers in sight. It seemed that most people were next door, in the other room, busy buying 1-1 sessions with clairvoyants or having a massage.

Business was slow and a few of them were worried they could not afford to pay for their stall by the end of the weekend event. They needed to make sales.

I approached two guys on different stalls. One was selling aromatherapy oils, and the other shamanic drums and jewellery. I said I would try a little experiment for one hour. I played the whole nine Solfeggio tones through my PA speakers on a very low volume, and as predicted, within one hour, both stall holders were three lengths deep in customers desperate to look at and buy their products. Both guys gave me a 'thumbs up' and a big smile of gratitude as the tones had completely altered and changed the mood of the room.

Then, one time, a young deaf and blind girl entered one of my music workshops, linking her mother's arm. I couldn't help but wonder how she would experience these tones. With a curious eye, I watched her closely.

To my amazement, she remained very still with her feet lightly tapping on the wooden floor, with a big beautiful smile across her face. As the session finished, I approached the mother and asked her if she could share with me her daughter's experience.

In awe, I watched how the daughter communicated her feelings through hand signals with her mother, their hands locked into a silent sign language between them both. The mother translated her daughter's delight with the session, she said she really enjoyed it. What had touched her heart most, though, were the sensations of the tones vibrating under her feet and then resonating throughout her entire being, bringing up feelings of joy and happiness. I was so excited, as this was a glowing testimonial of how these tones really work. You don't hear them. You FEEL them!

The eighth digital healing tone is 852 Hz, is based at the third eye energy centre, and is all about 'Transforming and Raising Awareness.' This tone can elevate your consciousness, build your intuition and deepen your connection to the spiritual realms.

Reflect: Imagine what steps you can take to enhance your awareness and foster greater alignment with yourself, others, animals, and the planet.

Use the space here to write (or in your journal) about the type of music you love, and why you love it. Have you ever listened to music that uplifts you? How is it different from other songs? What thoughts, ideas, and insights came up for you while reading this chapter?

_____

_____

_____

_____

_____

_____

_____

_____

_____

_____

_____

Elyse Unveiled: A Captivating Photoshoot. Embodying Elyse's Essence and Branding

Making Memories: David, Sheila Gott and Me at The Windmill Pub, Denton 2019

9

THE REUNION AND
MY SOLO CAREER!

In 2016, an unexpected reconnection took me back into the world of 90s music, setting the stage for an exciting new journey. The divine meeting began when I resumed communication with the original MAXX music producer based in Berlin, Germany and by the following year, I found myself performing live at some of the 90s music festivals across the world again.

After a long break spanning over twenty-three years, the stage was set in August of 2017 with a new booking agent and gigs confirmed in Estonia and Finland over one weekend, with Peru and Germany the following month. The high of performing in MAXX again, combined with the sheer joy of connecting with thousands of loyal 90s music enthusiasts, turned this chapter of my musical journey into a dream come true. As fate would have it, not only did the original producer and I renew our working relationship, but we also agreed for me to interview and find a new male rapper. Initially, it was a challenge as MAXX's distinctive style involves delivering rap in a reggae fashion, a rather uncommon approach. However, after a series of attempts, I eventually discovered a fantastic rapper who has been working alongside me since 2018.

Something I have found really interesting during this time is that there are some MAXX fans who continue to call me by my old name of Linda, but what really warms my heart is that there are some sweet souls who have lovingly embraced my new artist name, Elyse. Their support and openness to this new name change fills my heart with gratitude.

These days, you'll find me enjoying the spotlight at countless 90s music festivals, nightclubs, and cruise ships. From there, I do interviews on TV, radio, and podcasts worldwide, basking in the joy of reliving the 90s era again. I also really enjoy connecting with fans on social media, and I love meeting face-to-face to sign autograph cards and capture special moments in photos as well.

This reunion has brought not just 90s music but a renewed sense of purpose and joy back into my life, and it feels absolutely fantastic to be back.

Sadly though in January 2018, my world took an unexpected turn when I experienced the heartbreaking loss of my beautiful stepfather, Harry. His sudden departure was an extremely depressing time that completely overturned my life in ways I hadn't foreseen. I had to go through a tough grieving process because not only had he been a major influence in my life, he had accepted me as his own and he was my 'real' father, my Dad. He had been together with my mum for over forty two years and so his passing left a big empty hole for both of us. Thankfully, my mum and I were by his side during his final moments, and for that, I am truly grateful. Losing someone close to you makes you realise how delicate and valuable life is, reminding us not to take it for granted and enjoy every moment.

MY SOLO CAREER

When the world shut down in 2020, I took the time out to rest and completely recharge. With no flights to catch, hotels to sleep in or shows to perform at, I saw it as the perfect opportunity to not only chill out, but to focus on my solo music again. It had been a while since I had released my first album in May 2015, so it definitely felt like the right time.

Before delving into the music, I began researching and studying online courses on business, nutrition, wealth, sound healing, and other frequencies. I thought this might help me learn how to manage my solo business more effectively, especially in terms of online promotion and creating more digital products to sell.

I found out that besides the widely recognised 9 Solfeggio frequencies (along with the popular 432 Hz), there are many other tones such as the angelic frequencies of 111, 222, 333, 444, 555, 666, 777, 888, and 999 Hz. Additionally, I stumbled upon some other interesting tones like 110, 295.8, and 415 Hz—completely mind-blowing!

By 2021 I had written and released a couple of new

singles, started to plan my second album idea and successfully developed a nine module online course which I called 'The Love Energy Frequency' program. This program was filmed over two full days with a professional video team in my mum's front living room. With my hair and make-up done I managed to film over 54 short videos into camera (with a teleprompter) and I had a great time creating it. It was so much fun.

Creating this course has made me feel really happy and I'm so grateful for all the program members who joined. And I can't wait for the newcomers too!

It soon came around to 2022 and I thought about writing a book about my life's journey so far and most importantly I wanted to share how amazing these digital healing tones had made such a big difference in my life. They have not only helped me heal, but have helped others in their healing journey too. I had also managed to do a couple of solo gigs around the UK too.

And now having reached my mature years, I've come to appreciate that I've been blessed with a wealth of wisdom. Unlike the crazy, hectic long working days of the 90s, I now organise my time with ease and manage stress and fame with a whole new attitude. Making self-care a top priority has become crucial to my overall well-being. I've implemented a new daily routine where I engage in meditation while listening to a variety of frequency tones in the background on a low volume. It's a practice that not only aligns my heart and soul, but also serves as a source of renewed positive energy.

I have found that these specially created guided meditations and tones that I have personally created, contribute to my overall well-being, helping me gain a sense of inner peace and a better healthier connection to myself.

My approach to relationships has evolved too – nurtured by experience, they are now grounded in a deeper understanding, making healthier connections that endure the test of time. The contrast between my younger self and now is not just time-related, but reflective of my own personal healing journey marked by my resilience, and a profound appreciation for the balance between success and personal well-being.

I was extremely busy in 2023 laying down the foundations for this book, completing my second album 'Feel The Love' and singing at events again where I had first started back in 2013, ten years ago.

I also reconnected with my birth father, Pepe, who I haven't seen since I was five years old. He now lives in Florida and although we haven't met in person since that time, we had a brief chat and I'm looking forward to the possibility of meeting him again one day soon.

These days though, you'll find me out on long nature walks or chilling at home drinking green tea with my other half David and our playful four-year-old cat 'Cheeky Boy' (trust me, he lives up to that name!). We're still living in Manchester, however we've got big dreams of travelling to America as part of our work.

LOVE ENERGY MUSIC

My ultimate goal is to spread love and good vibes worldwide. I believe that music can be energising, empowering and change how you feel for the better, it just needs motivating lyrics and better frequency tuning that's all.

My mission doesn't stop there, I plan to build a whole new music industry by transforming old churches into music hub centres for healing and I would like to invite you to be a part of it too. Your support means the world to me and I hope you continue to follow my journey. Together, let's create a musical revolution that spreads love, compassion, and peace. Thank you for being a part of this incredible journey to love energy with me and embracing the nine digital healing tones. I hope you've enjoyed it as much as I have enjoyed creating it for you.

The ninth digital healing tone is 963 Hz, is based at the crown energy centre, and is all about 'Awakening Perfect State and Oneness'. This tone creates a sense of unity with the universe and all living beings. Assists in transcending the limitations of the ego and the material world.

Reflect: What practices or experiences can help you attain a state of perfect oneness, bringing you closer to a sense of wholeness and unity?

Use the space here to write (or in your journal) how you feel now after embarking on this journey. How can you get into oneness with all living beings? What thoughts, ideas and insights came up for you while reading this last chapter?

_____
_____
_____
_____
_____
_____
_____

FREE RESOURCE: Your free 9 digital healing tones: https://elysemusic.com/bookbonus

MAXX Reunion: A 23-Year Hiatus Ends! Elyse Singing Live At The 02 Arena, Wembley, London 2018

2023 Reflections: Embracing Solitude in a Captivating Solo Photoshoot

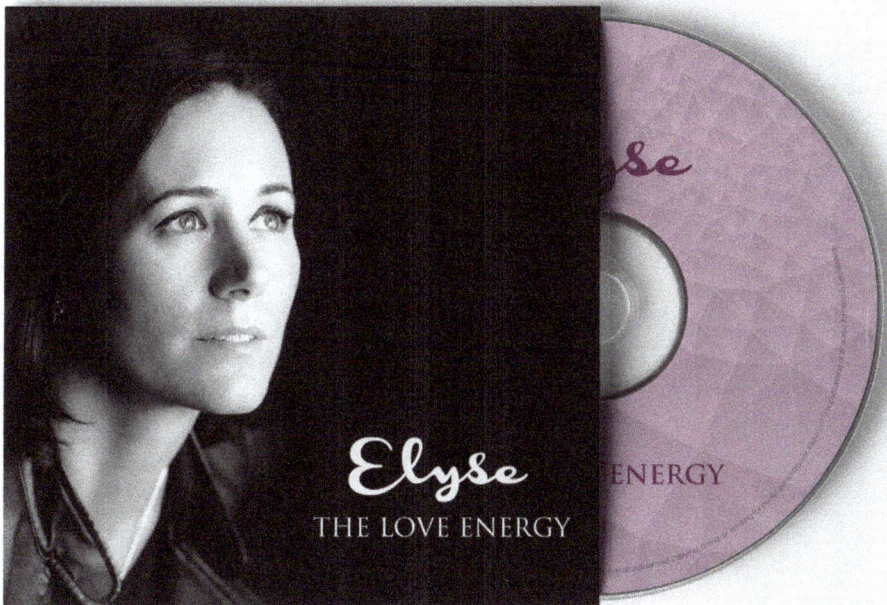

My First Album 'The Love Energy'
Available In Both Digital & Physical Formats From: www.elysemusic.com

'The 9 Solfeggio Frequency' Album Available In Both Digital & Physical Formats
From: www.elysemusic.com

My 2nd Album 'Feel The Love' is now Available
on all digital platforms and my www.elysemusic.com

EPILOGUE

YOUR JOURNEY BEGINS

Now, as we come to the end of this transformative journey together, remember that you hold the keys to your own vibrational fate. By embracing these nine digital healing tones, you've unlocked the doors to a world of loving energy. Your energy centres are now beginning to flow more freely, getting you into harmony with your own unique vibration.

Decide right now what music enters your ears. Will it be the standard music tuned to 440 Hz, or will you listen to something different from now on? The choice is yours.

The truth is you are not bound by an old narrative anymore. You no longer need to listen to sorrowful, unloving lyrics and lower-based frequencies that drag you down. What you need now, more than ever, is music that elevates your spirit, restores your faith, and wraps you in love.

In a world bursting with many super-talented songwriters, each with their own gifts and beliefs, my wish is that they start to write songs with more positive lyrics, all tuned to a happier frequency.

This book is not only about frequencies, though, it's about self-discovery and love. It's about my journey to love and how I am where I am today because of these powerful tones.

I've learned that the purest form of love starts from within. And it is through these frequencies, these vibrations of love, that I found the strength to embrace every part of myself, to release the judgments, and to let self-love flow.

So now, I invite you to reflect on your own journey.

Remember, you are a soul, and wherever your energy is right now, it can be lifted even higher. The fact that you're here today is a testament to your inner strength. I'm incredibly proud of you.

It's time to let your love energy shine bright, lighting up the world and the world of those around you.

May you, dear reader, find inspiration in my journey. May you embrace the power of self-love and allow it to guide you through life's challenges. May the harmonious melodies of the digital healing tones continue to resonate within you, reminding you of your inherent worth and right to be here.

With boundless love energy,

Elyse
♥

Elyse & David: Embracing Elegance and Intimacy at a Black Tie Event, London Dec 2021.

ABOUT ELYSE G. ROGERS

Born in Manchester, UK, Elyse G. Rogers discovered her musical calling at the age of 14 when she lent her soulful voice to a funk and soul band with a group of friends. In 1994, she had a remarkable journey with the German Eurodance group MAXX, experiencing top ten hits globally, which propelled Elyse into the spotlight, with TV and radio appearances, music videos shot in Marseille, Budapest, and New York, and world tours. In 2017, Elyse returned to the international stage, touring once again with MAXX.

Today, Elyse is not just a seasoned artist but a passionate supporter of positive music and the transformative potential of digital healing tones. Her debut album, 'The Love Energy,' released in 2015, harmoniously aligns all nine tracks with the 9 Solfeggio tones. This musical journey is backed by 'The Love Energy Frequency' online program, a comprehensive nine-week module course designed to impart knowledge and empower individuals to seamlessly integrate these uplifting tones into their lives with joy. Her latest offering, a new second album, is a testament to her continued dedication, available for streaming on digital platforms and for purchase on her website in both digital and physical formats.

Elyse Music helps spiritual seekers and music enthusiasts raise their vibrational energy to the frequency of love through love-energy music. Enabling the audience to achieve a euphoric state of self-confidence and inner peace, so they can manifest their highest potential without the fear of energetic stagnation or the struggle of navigating their spiritual journey alone.

On the 21st of May 2015, 'The Love Energy' album was released, coinciding with mine and David's eight-year wedding anniversary. It's been incredibly well-received, continuing to sell both digitally and in physical copies, with a dedicated fanbase worldwide. Additionally, I've crafted 'The 9 Solfeggio Frequency' CD and, more recently, a second album, titled: 'Feel The Love' released on 21st May 2024, with a third album in the works, alongside EPs, singles and some major collaborations already in progress.

This album - as well as all of my other music and my online course, The love Energy Frequency Program - is available at: https://elysemusic.com/

ELYSE on social media:
https://www.youtube.com/@elysemusicuk/videos
https://www.instagram.com/elysemusicuk/
https://www.facebook.com/elysemusicuk/
https://www.tiktok.com/elysemusicuk

MAXX on YouTube:
https://www.youtube.com/@maxxmusic90s/videos

A few years ago, I discovered that my husband David is a Heyoka Empath, which is one of the rarest and most powerful healers on the planet. Using humour, he acts as a spiritual mirror to those around him to assist in their growth.

If you would like to know more, visit David's website: https://www.davidianrogers.com/

THE LOVE ENERGY FREQUENCY TRANSFORMATION

CONTENT

01 02 03 04 05

MODULE 1
The History of Music
440 Hz
Solfeggio Frequencies
Energy Centres
Intention
Frequency 1 - 174 Hz

MODULE 2
Aura
5 Easy Ways to Clean Your Aura
Its All About the Vibe
Vibrational Frequency Chart
Frequency 2 - 285 Hz

MODULE 3
Sound Waves
Human Body Frequency
Earth Frequency
Different Frequencies
Frequency 3 - 396 Hz

MODULE 4
Lets talk about Stress
Emotions
The Body Atlas Map
Church Organ
Frequency 4 - 417 Hz

MODULE 5
Soul Alignment
The Love Energy
Water Crystals
DNA
Frequency 5 - 528 Hz

Modules 1-5 - 'The Love Energy Frequency Transformation Program'

THE LOVE ENERGY FREQUENCY TRANSFORMATION

CONTENT

06 07 08 09 10

MODULE 6
Map of Consciousness
Healing with Colours
Forgiveness Prayer
Frequency Medicine
Frequency 6 - 639 Hz

MODULE 7
Planet Alignment
Focus
Authentic Self
Electromagnetic
Frequency 7 - 741 Hz

MODULE 8
Binaural Beats
Tuning Forks
Sound Bowls
Cymatics
Frequency 8 - 852 Hz

MODULE 9
Vitruvian Man
The meaning of 3, 6, 9
Malta & The Pyramids
Elevate
Frequency 9 - 963 Hz

BONUS
The Power of 432 Hz
Foods that Vibrate
Money Frequency
AM FM Radio
295.8 Hz

Modules 6-9 with Bonus - 'The Love Energy Frequency Transformation Program'